FRIDA KAHLO

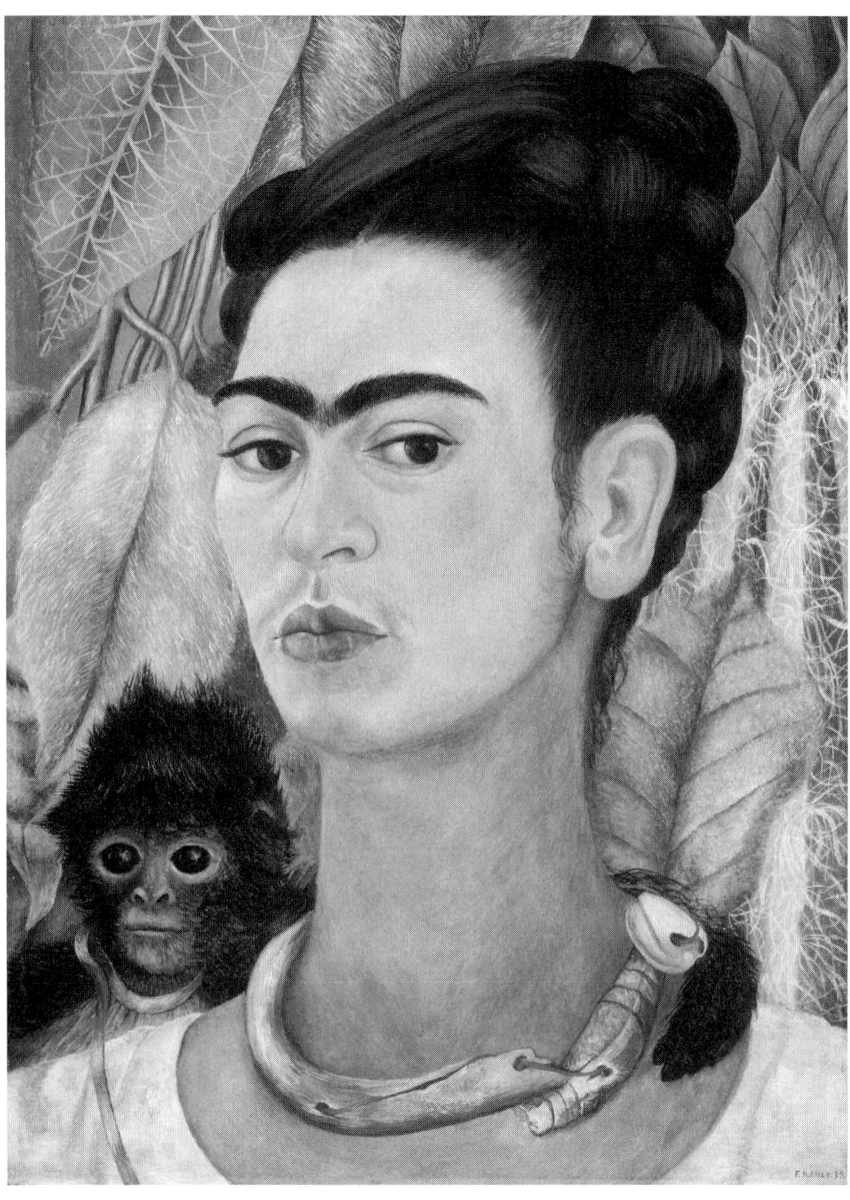

Frida Kahlo, Self Portrait with Monkey. *1938, oil on Masonite, support: 12 × 16" (30.48 × 40.64 cm.). Albright-Knox Art Gallery, Buffalo, New York. Bequest of A. Conger Goodyear, 1966. © 2008 Banco de México Diego Rivera & Frida Kahlo Museums Trust. Av. Cinco de Mayo No.2, Col. Centro, Del. Cuauhtémoc 06059, México, D.F.*

FRIDA KAHLO

A Biography

Claudia Schaefer

GREENWOOD BIOGRAPHIES

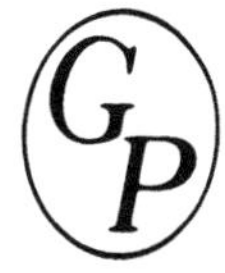

GREENWOOD PRESS
WESTPORT, CONNECTICUT • LONDON

Library of Congress Cataloging-in-Publication Data

Schaefer, Claudia, 1949-
Frida Kahlo : a biography / Claudia Schaefer.
p. cm. — (Greenwood biographies, ISSN 1540–4900)
Includes bibliographical references and index.
ISBN 978–0–313–34924–9 (alk. paper)
1. Kahlo, Frida. 2. Painters—Mexico—Biography. I. Title.
ND259.K33S33 2009
759.972—dc22
[B] 2008036704

British Library Cataloguing in Publication Data is available.

Library of Congress Catalog Card Number: 2008036704
ISBN: 978–0–313–34924–9
ISSN: 1540–4900

First published in 2009

Greenwood Press, 88 Post Road West, Westport, CT 06881
An imprint of Greenwood Publishing Group, Inc.
www.greenwood.com

Printed in the United States of America

The paper used in this book complies with the Permanent Paper Standard issued by the National Information Standards Organization (Z39.48–1984).

10 9 8 7 6 5 4 3 2 1

CONTENTS

SERIES FOREWORD

In response to high school and public library needs, Greenwood developed this distinguished series of full-length biographies specifically for student use. Prepared by field experts and professionals, these engaging biographies are tailored for high school students who need challenging yet accessible biographies. Ideal for secondary school assignments, the length, format and subject areas are designed to meet educators' requirements and students' interests.

Greenwood offers an extensive selection of biographies spanning all curriculum-related subject areas including social studies, the sciences, literature and the arts, history and politics, as well as popular culture, covering public figures and famous personalities from all time periods and backgrounds, both historic and contemporary, who have made an impact on American and/or world culture. Greenwood biographies were chosen based on comprehensive feedback from librarians and educators. Consideration was given to both curriculum relevance and inherent interest. The result is an intriguing mix of the well known and the unexpected, the saints and sinners from long-ago history and contemporary pop culture. Readers will find a wide array of subject choices from fascinating crime figures like Al Capone to inspiring pioneers like Margaret Mead, from the greatest minds of our time like Stephen Hawking to the most amazing success stories of our day like J.K. Rowling.

While the emphasis is on fact, not glorification, the books are meant to be fun to read. Each volume provides in-depth information about the subject's life from birth through childhood, the teen years, and adulthood.

A thorough account relates family background and education, traces personal and professional influences, and explores struggles, accomplishments, and contributions. A timeline highlights the most significant life events against a historical perspective. Bibliographies supplement the reference value of each volume.

ACKNOWLEDGMENTS

I have spent over two decades studying Frida Kahlo's life and art. During that time, there has been lots of planned research and travel to Mexico City and especially to the Blue House to see art and buildings firsthand, study Frida's library, and breathe the air of Coyoacán from inside her enclosed patio. I thank Raúl Rodríguez-Hernández for his patience in going to all of these places without complaint. Even more: I thank him for his patience each time I interrupted his own work with a cry of "guess what I found out about her now?"

There have been just as many unexpected encounters with Frida that have contributed to my knowledge and to this book. This includes an invitation from the Tate Modern in London in 2005 to revisit all things Frida, and one from Jorge Volpi to join a tremendous crowd of Frida enthusiasts at the National Museum of Anthropology in Mexico City in the summer of 2007 at an event named after a new film about her life called *Yo soy Frida* (I am Frida). I am grateful for both of these invitations; they have kept me aware of the latest takes on Frida. Twenty years is a long time to stay ahead of the curve, and both of these experiences have been invaluable.

I am grateful to my editor at Greenwood, Debra Adams, who approached me with a question about my interest in doing this biography. At the time, I wasn't sure. After spending another year plus with Frida, I am happy to say I thank Debra for contacting me. Writing this has been a great experience, which I hope comes through in my tone. I hope that this book brings a new understanding of Frida to old and new audiences.

INTRODUCTION

There are as many versions of the life of Mexican artist Frida Kahlo as there are biographers. Tracing the details of her 47 years is both entertaining and frustrating, since so much of what is known has been passed down in stories and even some tall tales. It is a hard task to sift through historical documents, personal letters, the remembrances of friends, and the handwritten comments left by the artist herself to try to figure out what actually happened and what has been embellished. There are many overlaps between different versions of the same story but, in the end, what matters most is that "Frida," the recognizable face of the woman Frida Kahlo, is greater than the sum total of all of these fragments and contradictions. She is both what she did and what is said about her. Frida's husband, Mexican artist Diego Rivera, took it upon himself to invent larger than life characters for both of them, and Frida followed his lead with additions of her own. Accounts of how radical and shocking Rivera's contributions to the nightlife of Mexico's artistic scene were, or how spiteful and flagrant Frida's revenge on his womanizing was, vary according to the storyteller and the audience.

Like the history of modern Mexico, a nation that came into being around the same time that Frida was born, there is a lot of myth that complements and enriches plain facts. Cultures constantly renegotiate their ideas, beliefs, and customs, and this holds true for individuals as it does for communities. Modern though it may have been, Mexico in the decades of the twentieth century after the Revolution that began in 1910 was still built on a combination of the myths of revolutionary change and democratic rule, and the traditional foundational values inherited from a more distant past. This was as true during Frida's lifetime (1907–1954) as it would be in the following decades. When the federal government headquartered in the capital began a tremendous financial investment in the architectural and social development of Mexico City in the 1950s, a clash between old and new myths was evident. The downtown center of the city was the site for the construction of landmark buildings such as the *Torre Latinoamericana* or Latin American Tower, opened in 1956, the tallest skyscraper in Latin America and the tallest building in Mexico since the International Capital Building of 1935 (which it greatly surpassed). Foreign architects were brought in to construct the business and residential buildings that were visible evidence of the economic boom of the 1940s and 1950s. This international cooperation was proof that Mexico belonged on the world stage as a metropolitan city. Yet a few kilometers outside the city sat the Pyramid of the Sun and the Pyramid of the Moon, connected by a still unexcavated Avenue of the Dead. These vestiges of the city of Teotihuacan, Aztec but with tributary contributions by the Totonac, Otomi, Zapotec, Mixtec, Maya and Nahua cultures, survived alongside the newest marvels of construction. Literature and the arts in Mexico over the same historical period—roughly 1910 through the 1950s and 1960s—reflect similar parallels. The novels of Carlos Fuentes and the murals of Diego Rivera, the paintings of Frida Kahlo and the photographs of Tina Modotti, the art of Remedios Varo, and the stories of Juan Rulfo, all come together in a universe of competing myths and legends to contribute to what will become Mexico. The life of Frida Kahlo is no less energized and enhanced by the stories told about her or woven in her own words around her self-portraits. Her earliest scenes show women dressed in traditional indigenous clothing sitting in buses next to women in silk stockings and short skirts. As Frida and Mexico came of age, they worked out the ways they would deal with these dual elements.

As a young girl, Frida Kahlo lived at the crossroads of many challenges. This began with her parents, who came from two very different backgrounds and cultures, then polio, then her defiant act of going to school in the city, followed by a violent traffic accident that would change the course of her life forever. The earliest demands on her came from her mother Matilde, who tried to raise Frida and her sisters according to the older, provincial ways she had learned in her native Oaxaca. A rebel from the start, Frida coped with her father's melancholic temperament better than she did with her mother's strict discipline. The time her father Guillermo spent in his studio or taking photographs around Mexico City seemed infinitely more inviting to the young Frida than learning the tasks of women at home. She began to dream of imaginary friends who could escape from daily life. When her father offered her a chance to continue her education beyond the local German school nearby, that dream came true. She saw the *Prepa* or preparatory school as an open door, and she ran through it. Just like Mexican culture ran toward modernity, Frida saw her future among those at the school. Once the city lay at her feet to discover, Frida never looked back.

From adolescence and through her early adult years, Frida made a name for herself as a woman who would not fit easily into a single mold. Her older sisters were conservative and dressed that way, her younger sister Cristina dressed according to the latest styles, but Frida took on different identities with different types of clothing. She put on men's clothing when it suited her; she wore pants when it was not common for women; she adopted indigenous shawls, skirts, and blouses. Frida was "Mexican" in that she combined so many traditions in one. And she could call attention to herself in any crowd. On Fifth Avenue in New York City, on the streets of Paris, or upon entering an auditorium in Mexico City for a classical music concert, people stopped in their tracks when they saw her. Frida's colorful outfits, her Mexican jewelry, her hair ribbons and long skirts, and the French perfume she doused herself with created an image that was hard to ignore, and even harder to forget.

Frida was barely out of her teens when she met muralist Diego Rivera, who was working on art commissions near her school. Maybe as a sign of rebellion, maybe as an adolescent crush, Frida declared her love for this man almost two decades older than she was. Some of the myths surrounding the life of Frida have to do with her relationship with Diego, some with other men and women who came into her life, and some with her own fantasies. If nothing else, Diego was the catalyst for Frida learning the lesson that growing up meant sacrifice and pain even as it brought companionship or, perhaps, love.

When she died in 1954 just days after her birthday, Frida Kahlo was already a popular figure in Mexican society, well known at home and in art circles in general. She had been the teacher of a group of talented young artists, the wife of an important painter, and had even had a one-woman show in a modern art gallery in Mexico City in 1953. Still, she was not yet a superstar. How much her reputation would grow over the following five decades was perhaps unpredictable at the time because her husband, government-sponsored public artist Diego Rivera, occupied the spotlight more often. His work, his life, and even the 1949 autobiography he wrote in a fairly flamboyant style all captured the attention of men and women before they turned to look at her. This would happen quickly, however.

Her artwork—especially the numerous self-portraits Frida painted as she convalesced from serious illnesses and a dreadful accident in 1925—was one aspect of her rapid acceptance by audiences around the world, but the details of her life, cut short tragically at the age of 47, soon expanded popular interest in her. Since then, Frida Kahlo has come to be known as "Frida," an indicator of how close people feel to her and how much they empathize with her. Everything about Frida Kahlo has become a symbol: her immigrant father, her childhood sickness, her near death in the accident, her early marriage to the strong-willed Rivera, her romances at home and abroad, her identity between cultures, her artistic expression, and even her open sexuality all mean more than meets the eye.

Everyone who comes to Frida's story brings one of their own, and there are so many aspects to her life that it is almost inevitable that matches will be found or empathy aroused. Frida's life and her art are accessible to anyone. Her experiences are not limited to a single time and place but are much more cross-cultural as part of a shared sense of modern life. Anyone might emigrate, be the victim of a vehicle accident, suffer from disease or illness, be jealous of others, or have a less than perfect marriage. One need not be an art historian to appreciate her paintings either. Her self-portraits—the type of painting Frida produced the most—have all the requirements of technique, color, style, line, and the like; at the same time, they strip away the outer surface to reveal the inner person. This is the point where external challenges meet internal strength. At her lowest, Frida looks like a victim. At her best, she is a survivor. And these are the human qualities that have attracted audiences to her from all cultures and all parts of the world.

The influences on Frida were many: her family, her fellow students, European and American artists, friends, photographers, models, actresses, financiers, physicians. Some have called her a Surrealist painter, others a painter of the Americas. Some have called her a frustrated mother; others have seen her as a headstrong woman. Maybe all of these are true. In turn, she has influenced just as many categories of people from north and south of the Mexican border, from working classes to middle classes, from painters and weavers to tattoo artists. Her accomplishments were both personal and professional at a time when women tended to remain less visible than men were in the public sphere. Her struggles shadow those of contemporary men and women who live out the hope and despair of a world not unlike hers. The face of Frida is an icon, a likeness with significance beyond the literal. Her steady gaze, facing us in the good and the bad times, symbolizes the qualities needed to endure, and even to prevail. There is no universal one-fits-all Frida; she is what each of us makes of her. So, as the central figure of this book, Frida Kahlo is but one thread woven into an ongoing story of women and art and happiness and courage and disappointment and loss, one that begins at the dawn of the twentieth century but one that we have carried into the twenty-first.

TIMELINE: EVENTS IN THE LIFE OF FRIDA KAHLO

1872 Frida's father, Carl Wilhelm Kahlo, the son of a jeweler and photographer, is born in Baden-Baden, Germany to Jakob Heinrich Kahlo and Henriette E. Kaufmann. Frida claimed Hungarian Jewish ancestry for her father, but others have found evidence of his family being Lutheran. Her paternal grandmother was Romanian, part of a family of Jewish immigrants that moved to Germany. Photography, jewelry, and music were Carl Wilhelm's talents. Becoming deaf later in life, he could no longer hear the piano melodies he played for others.

1876 Frida's mother, Matilde Calderón y González, is born in Oaxaca to military man and photographer Antonio Calderón and a very devoutly religious mother, Isabel González.

1886 December 8: Diego Rivera is born in Guanajuato, Mexico.

1891 Wilhelm emigrates from Germany to Mexico after the death of his mother. His father's remarriage creates family problems, and he finds that stories of successful ventures in Mexico abound. He hears and reads of the chance to make a new life in Mexico and leaves home for good. His ship lands in Veracruz and from there he makes his way to Mexico City to find work.

1894 Wilhelm, whose name has now been rendered into Spanish as Guillermo, marries María Cerdeña. They have two daughters, but María dies in childbirth with the second in 1898.

1898 February 21: Guillermo Kahlo waits only a few months to marry native of Oaxaca Matilde Calderón y González, a *mestiza* of indigenous Mexican and European blood. Both Guillermo and Matilde had worked in a jewelry store together, and they had been close friends for a long time. Theirs is not a passionate romance, but is a relationship of mutual support. They have five children, but one (a son) dies as an infant. The sisters are Matilde, Adriana, Frieda (later Frida), and Cristina.

1899–1900 Guillermo becomes a photographer and compiles an album of commercial shots for a local business. His style is documentary and exact, capturing the process of the construction of buildings and the details of the architectural ornamentation of the new constructions in the so-called Mexican modern style.

1901 Guillermo Kahlo opens a studio as a professional photographer in the heart of the oldest part of downtown Mexico City. His work includes mostly buildings and urban streets, with very few portrait studies. He will dedicate himself to this profession through the 1920s. Afflicted since childhood with epilepsy, Guillermo needs help hauling his heavy photographic equipment around from place to place. He will enlist his favorite daughter—Frida—to accompany him on these excursions, in spite of her own struggle with polio. Maybe he saw them as kindred spirits and wanted to make her see she that could do anything in life despite adverse conditions and challenges.

1903–04 Frida's father builds the *Casa Azul* (Blue House) in Coyoacán, on the outskirts of Mexico City, for his new wife and family. Amid other new residences, this property will form the nucleus for the growth of the small, picturesque town.

1904–08 Guillermo Kahlo is hired by the government of Porfirio Díaz as the official photographer of state monuments and public works projects. His enthusiasm for taking shots of buildings rather than people produces a good number of albums and collections that document the development of modern public works promoted by the state. Examples of these photographs include the album *Mexiko 1904*, which portrays a growing city whose radiant streets, water works, neighborhoods, parks, lagoons, public squares, and gardens have an almost dreamlike quality, as if the official government image was just an illusion. Mexico City is, in his album, a Porfirian ideal being built before everyone's eyes. Foreign investment and material prosperity took the place of social justice or concern for the lower classes.

1907 July 6: At one o'clock in the morning, the Blue House welcomes a new addition to the Kahlo-Calderón family: Magdalena Carmen Frieda. She is their third daughter. After the Nazis come to power, she changes the German spelling to the more acceptable, Spanish-looking "Frida." The date of her birth will be changed and romanticized by Frida later in life, and she will be "reborn" to accompany the year of the Mexican Revolution (1910) in the myth she weaves around herself. Of course, this would also make her three years younger than she was.

1908 Frida's younger sister Cristina is born. She will later on turn out to be a second, irresistible object of affection for Diego, and he will include her portrait on the face of a worker in the mural he paints for the National Palace. Frida's face is on the woman standing behind Cristina's figure in the mural, a fact neither fails to notice.

1910 The Mexican Revolution begins. The government of dictator Porfirio Díaz (1876–1911)—known in popular terms as the Porfiriato—strives to modernize Mexico, often at the expense of human rights and freedom for the less wealthy classes. A proponent of the idea of no-reelection for any politician, Díaz finally calls for the country to vote. Of course, he nominates himself to run. Francisco I. Madero decided to run against Díaz. Afraid of Madero's popularity, Díaz has him thrown in jail and declares himself the winner. Madero flees to the United States, later returning to contest the results of the election as a fraud against the people. On November 20, 1910, Madero starts the Mexican Revolution. Skirmishes and battles take place across the nation, with the residential town of Coyoacán close but not in the center of the action in the big city.

1911 Madero is declared the winner of the election and takes office. Two years later, he is assassinated.

1913 At home in Coyoacán, in her first struggle with adversity, Frida's right leg begins to shrink and wither, most likely from polio, a fairly common disease at the time. She gets the nickname *Pata de Palo* (Peg Leg) from school friends and begins a lifelong quest to hide this physical deformity, even as she uses the same phrase to refer to herself when among friends. Long skirts do the trick, and their exotic look gives her a growing mystique as well. Frida begins what will often be a solitary life and creates imaginary friends who accompany her on the Alice-in-Wonderland-like adventures she conjures up. What her legs will not permit her to do, Frida fantasizes about. Suffering from epilepsy, her father calls upon her to help him lug his heavy camera equipment from shoot to shoot. He does not baby her, and she rises to the occasion by traveling with him far and wide around Mexico's growing cities of the central plateau.

1917 A modern constitution is approved for Mexico; it continues in effect—with some modifications—to this day. Frida and her school friends are adolescents during the heady years after the Revolution, when the future is filled with promise for them all.

1922 At a time when girls rarely attend classes beyond grade school, Guillermo recognizes Frida's intelligence and sends her to the select, mostly male *Escuela Nacional Preparatoria* (National Preparatory School). Her father envisions her preparing for college; her mother finds this outrageous and inappropriate since there are only a few girls among hundreds of young men. Frida declares an interest in medicine and shows talent for medical drawings. This is a turning point in her life: she makes new friends, meets influential families, and most of all sets eyes on Diego Rivera (already a national figure in the arts) as he paints the building's murals.

The idea of the Revolution, then, introduces a new kind of art for Mexico and a new relationship for Frida. She declares herself in love with him at first sight and announces to her friends that she will marry Diego. The weaving of her legend continues with this added character. Often an outsider, Frida is a rebel in her dress—sometimes austere and other times men's clothing—and in her behavior. She also invents a language all her own—*fridesco*—based on popular sayings mixed with foreign words and phrases heard at home, as well as colloquial language, jokes, and puns. She and several other young men form the group they call *los cachuchas*, a mix of intellectuals and practical jokers that spend their time exchanging challenges about readings they have done, political jabs, and pure camaraderie. The term *cachuchas* is a reference to the men's sport caps they all wear, but it is also a slang term referring to their shared student craziness, as visible as the headgear. They were expert intellectual debaters as much as practical jokers.

1925 September 17: On her way home from the Preparatory School one day, fate is not on Frida's side. A violent crash between an old-fashioned trolley and the modern bus she is riding in almost kills her. Reports abound in Mexico City of the girl covered in blood and gold dust—the glittery powder a nearby passenger was carrying that exploded upon impact—lying on the ground after the incident. Frida is gravely wounded; the result is a long period of recuperation in bed. Lying on her back, Frida has a special easel and pulley system rigged up to look at her face in the mirror and paint what she sees. Her use of self-portraits as therapy starts here. Frida sees the figure of death dancing around her bed and, later on, she fills the halls of the Blue House with Judas figures that echo this early trauma.

1926 Untrained in formal terms, Frida begins to teach herself to paint and develops her latent talent for art. From medical drawings, she turns to still lifes and portraits.

1928 Lured by Diego's political activities, Frida joins the Mexican Communist Party. She resigns in 1929, in support of Diego who is expelled by his comrades.

1929 August 21: Frida and Diego Rivera are married for the first time. Guillermo Kahlo warns Diego that Frida is something of a devil.

The *Partido Nacional Revolucionario* (National Revolutionary Party) is formed. It continues today as the *Partido Revolucionario Institucional* (Institutional Revolutionary Party) or the PRI. The party held power over the presidency until the elections of 2000, when Vicente Fox won for the *Partido de Acción Nacional* (National Action Party) or the conservative PAN party.

1930 November: Frida and Diego travel to San Francisco on his art commission from the California School of Fine Arts (now the San Francisco Art Institute). There, she meets photographer Edward Weston and strikes up a friendship with doctor Leo Eloesser, who is often paid with her artwork.

Weston's companion, Italian photographer Tina Modotti, becomes a close friend of Frida as well. (Later on, Modotti leaves Weston and moves permanently to Mexico City.) Frida undergoes multiple operations in the United States, all of her doctors promising to cure her physical problems with new procedures. Pain becomes a way of life for her.

1931 Frida and Diego return to Mexico City. Diego commissions the construction of two adjoining houses for them in the suburb of San Angel, connected by an elevated bridge. This allows them each a maximum of independence, despite being next-door neighbors. His continuing interest in other women, including Frida's sister Cristina, is coming between them. Diego never hides his extramarital affairs, but his tendency to exaggerate compounds Frida's difficulty in figuring out what is true and what is not. She puts up with a lot of gossip and storytelling in the meantime, and maybe even learns to counteract Diego's activities with some of her own adventures.

December 22: Diego is offered a solo retrospective exhibition at the newly opened Museum of Modern Art (MoMA) in New York City. The couple travels there together. Frida is introduced to high society and makes a name for herself by dressing as a *Tehuana* and parading up and down Fifth Avenue. It is difficult to overlook her exotic figure. She mocks high society and longs for Mexico, but she gains more admirers in New York.

1932 Frida and Diego spend time in Detroit while Diego works on murals of industrial scenes inside the Detroit Institute of Arts. Frida suffers her first miscarriage. She is admitted to the Henry Ford Hospital after her second miscarriage. Again, art becomes her therapy and she sketches detailed scenes of births and abortions. Frida's mother, Matilde Calderón, dies.

1933 Diego is commissioned to create a mural for the newly built Rockefeller Center in Manhattan. At his side, Frida is desperately homesick for Mexico. The strident themes and images of the mural offend the Rockefeller family, and Frida and Diego return to Mexico City in December. The murals are destroyed.

1937 Russian revolutionary Leon Trotsky is deported from the Soviet Union by Joseph Stalin. He seeks a place of exile.

Rejected as an immigrant by Norway, Trotsky approaches Rivera. Diego wins Trotsky's admission into Mexico. Trotsky arrives in the port of Tampico on January 11, 1937. Busy as always, Diego sends Frida to escort him to Coyoacán. She sets him up there in the Blue House with her father still in residence. Trotsky and his wife spend a lot of time together with Frida.

Frida has her first art show as part of a group exhibition in Mexico City.

1938 The Mexican petroleum industry is nationalized by President Lázaro Cárdenas. In a show of civic pride, Mexicans turn out in public to sell their dearest possessions to help support the bankrupt state. Frida adds to the effort by offering some of her flamboyant jewelry.

October: Frida is invited by New York gallery owner Julien Levy to display her paintings. Surrealist painter André Breton is taken with both Frida's art and personality. He invites her to Paris and, in a glowing tribute to her work, calls her a kind of natural Surrealist. In this way, Frida joins the ranks of other women painters like Remedios Varo, who are seen as being among the elite of the avant-garde.

1939 January: With a kidney infection and suffering more general ill health, Frida travels alone to Paris for the exhibit. Her work forms part of the group display called *Mexico* that includes pre-Columbian sculptures, folk art and, of course, some of her paintings. Diego wishes her well but stays in Mexico.

1939 Frida and Diego divorce. The reasons are not immediately clear but could very well have been related to his interest in so many other women and his absence from her professional life. Diego speaks well of Frida's work, but almost never joins her at exhibitions. Frida continues her close friendships with many men and women, some but not all in the field of art. Some of these friendships, like those with Japanese-American designer and sculptor Isamu Noguchi and Hungarian-born lithographer and photographer Nickolas Muray, are intimate.

1940 December 8: Frida and Diego remarry. Frida begins holding classes at the experimental school *La Esmeralda* for young artists such as muralist Arturo García Bustos. They are dubbed *Los Fridos* as her devoted students. These young male followers are very talented and will have successful careers in the arts, keeping Frida's legacy alive.

1940s Beginning in the middle of the decade, Frida begins to record sketches, thoughts, doubts, and pain in her diary. A volume of great debate, the diary reveals some of Frida's inner life but missing pages will hide parts of it that are only hinted at or, in some cases, denied, by those who knew her.

1941 April 14: Guillermo Kahlo dies in the Blue House.

1950 Frida's health worsens considerably. She is hospitalized for close to a year and suffers many complications.

1954 July 2: Frida, Diego, and other famous artists take to the streets to protest the CIA intervention in Guatemala's presidential elections. They rally for the left-wing winner, Jacobo Arbenz. This is the last time she is seen in public and she is seated in a wheelchair, looking thin and pale.

July 13: After many years of physical suffering, the amputation of a foot, and lengthy bouts with painkilling drugs, Frida dies in Mexico City. Diego is crushed. She is mourned in the auditorium of *El Palacio de Bellas Artes* (The Palace of Fine Arts) by hundreds of friends and influential politicians. Diego has her coffin draped in the Communist flag and this causes a commotion. Frida's remains are cremated, although she had resisted the idea. Her ashes are returned to the Blue House, inside a pre-Columbian urn; it is a very fitting place of rest since it is the home she has known for the longest. The ashes are later moved.

1957 November 24: Diego dies. One side of his body has been paralyzed for a couple of months, and a final heart attack does him in. He has been suffering from cancer as well, and his body no longer has any resistance to disease.

1958 July 12: The Blue House is opened to the public as a museum for the first time. Diego's museum-like house, filled with pre-Columbian artifacts, opens the same year to the general public.

1982 The Whitechapel Art Gallery in London is the site of the first celebration of the art of Frida Kahlo.

2005 The Tate Modern Museum in London sponsors an exhibit of Frida's works, the first collective one in thirty years. There is also a three-day conference at the Tate, bringing together art historians and other cultural critics to assess the developments related to the phenomenon of "Frida" since 1975.

2007 July 6: The discovery of a hidden room in the Blue House, one that contains over 22,000 documents, drawings, books, magazines, and sketches by both Frida and Diego, brings renewed interest in the artist and her work. To coincide with the Centennial celebration, items of clothing and all sorts of documents from this treasure trove go on display for the public starting in July. Her closet is opened, and the dresses she wears in her self-portraits are also put on display.

2007 The Palacio de Bellas Artes in Mexico City holds a special centennial exhibit and other events to commemorate the one hundredth anniversary of the birth of Frida Kahlo. San Diego and other places follow suit, with artists from Minneapolis doing works in her honor, theater groups in Dallas, Havana, and New York presenting aspects of her life, puppet shows opening in Mexico City, and a variety of other commemorative events taking place beginning in late summer.

Chapter 1

THE MYTH TAKES WING

In the five decades since her death, Frida Kahlo has become recognizable around the world. Her art adorns the mansions of Hollywood stars, she has been played in popular films by actresses Salma Hayek and Ofelia Medina, and she looks at us from the covers of matchbooks, erasers, the pockets of kitchen aprons, the covers of novels and cookbooks, wall clocks, pencil sharpeners, watchbands, and even Halloween masks. Popular altars in Mexico and in the American southwest often contain tiny *ex-votos*, or votive offerings, to saints or the divinity in gratitude for a cure performed, and some of these evoke Frida Kahlo as their intercessor. Pilgrims leave these small objects—made of silver or tin, or tiny painted figures of the person or part of the body that was healed—as testimony to health restored by intercession. They may include written texts explaining the miracle, or even symbols. The mutilation of Frida's body by surgical interventions and other procedures made her the perfect candidate for the companion of someone similarly afflicted. When she drew in her diary a pair of wings floating in mid-air or attached to her back after the amputation of her foot, Frida began a conversation with people steeped in popular rituals, who could identify with the substitution of flight for mere walking.

Frida's distinctive clothing—taken from the women of the Isthmus of Tehuantepec where the land barrier between the Gulf of Mexico and the Pacific Ocean is the smallest, and where both reality and myth give evidence of a strong and resistant matriarchal society—has inspired fashion designers, who have adapted her personal style into their ethnic dresses and jewelry. The peasant skirts and indigenous jewelry that contributed to her movie-star look are celebrated as both a sense of cultural style she inherited from Mexico and the hallmarks of a muse for her own time and long after. Long hair parted in the middle and swept up into braids fastened with flowers, clips, and ornaments adorn models on the runway and on the pages of style and leisure guides, especially those aimed at travelers interested in Mexico. Frida look-alikes grace the covers of high fashion magazines and home décor catalogues, staring out in unblinking defiance. From Neiman Marcus to Yves Saint Laurent and Saks Fifth Avenue, pieces of Frida are available on the fashion market for those who wish to evoke her style. Contrary to current health trends, however, the accompanying cigarette in the graceful hands of the model or even between her lips, a pose fairly common in later photographic portraits of Kahlo, does not give rise to as much emulation, even for the most independent women of the twenty-first century.

Represented and known through a close-up of her face, the historical person now familiar to us as just Frida floats across piles of items available for purchase, fills the walls of art galleries, and appears larger than life on the silver screen. For some, she is an inspiration; for others, a mystery. The real woman behind that mask lived a short 47 years, but they were years brimming with celebrations and challenges, triumphs and frustrations. One thing can be said about the life of Frida Kahlo: it was never dull or boring and sometimes it was overwhelming. Frida was born into a Mexico on the verge of great changes, a Mexico that had lived just over thirty years under the dictatorship of Porfirio Díaz and was ripe for democratic elections. Between the heat of politics and the heat of a midsummer day, Frida's arrival was connected to both turmoil and promise. Her life reflected those complex times.

Magdalena Carmen Frieda Kahlo y Calderón was born at one o'clock in the morning on July 6, 1907, in the idyllic town of Coyoacán in the center of the valley of Mexico. During the first decade of the twentieth century, what we now know as the metropolis of Mexico City only had about 400,000 inhabitants. At that time, it was a growing urban center surrounded by lush green gardens and open fields, perched on the vestiges of Lake Texcoco, which the Spanish had found when they first set foot there in the sixteenth century. It held convents, family estates, fruit orchards, and farms extending outwards into the valley, which was surrounded on all sides by tall mountains. All this vegetation would be developed, divided, and modernized in later decades, but in 1907 the air was still clean and clear and families enjoyed their small paradise. Coyoacán sits right on the edge of Mexico City, in Frida Kahlo's time at a stone's throw from it and now completely submerged by its expansion.

Frida Kahlo and her family were residents of that appealing enclave. When asked, Frida insisted on making the distinction that she was from Coyoacán and not from Mexico City. In 1907, this was an easier division to make than it is today. Located about an hour's drive from the beautiful *Palacio de Bellas Artes* (Palace of Fine Arts) in downtown Mexico City—give or take an hour or two depending on the time of day and the amount of traffic—Coyoacán is no longer a separate town, but a tree-lined series of streets and parks toward the south of that bustling metropolis, one of its sixteen boroughs. The reminder of a forgotten time, it is a bit quieter and less congested. Comfortable houses peek out from behind colorful walls, keeping the lives of their inhabitants more secluded and their activities more secret from the outside world than in the downtown. Incorporated into the city only in 1950, many streets are still paved with cobblestones. Small plazas, cafés, art galleries, bookstores, and restaurants beckon amid the stately mansions, including the house where Frida grew up, now a museum open to the public and filled with her paintings, kitchenware, canopied bed, library, and photographs. Founded on the shores of Lake Texcoco, on which Tenochtitlan—ancient Mexico City—was first built by the Aztecs and then rebuilt by the Spanish, Coyoacán is also home to preserved sixteenth-century cloisters and chapels, although the coyotes to which its name refers have long since disappeared. Runners and joggers find ample space for exercising, there are four movie houses, an arts center, and a commercial mall for shoppers interested in locally-produced arts or elegant, imported goods.

One hundred years ago, Frida would have had a totally different experience. Judging by her journal and many comments about the neighborhood, for her Coyoacán was where her imagination could run free. Its open spaces and small streets were the perfect place for children to play undisturbed. As a child, she lived in the comfortable *Casa Azul* (Blue House), which her father had built for his growing family and nearby were the school, churches, and park where she spent most of her time. Later, Coyoacán would become the space where she was confined by illness, far from her friends and schoolmates who congregated in downtown Mexico City. Looking back, Frida thought the town seemed both near and far away from all of the action and excitement going on in the city. In 1907, Mexico City was only a dream in the eyes of its urban planners, who envisioned the construction of boulevards using the broad avenues of Paris as a model. From the dictatorship of Porfirio Díaz onward, the government erected beautiful architecture, and kept sparkling reservoirs filled with clean drinking water.

A singularly solitary man, Frida's father Wilhelm (later Guillermo) Kahlo chose Coyoacán—the place of coyotes—for the construction of the family home. Formerly a parcel of land belonging to an estate passed down from generation to generation within one family, the area he built on was now broken up to allow new construction. The intensely green foliage and fresh air of the area's high altitude were attractive to new residents, and they came in droves. There was no better place for all of them to grow and prosper. For the new parents, hope filled the air.

An immigrant from Baden-Baden, Germany, Carl Wilhelm Kahlo arrived in Mexico attracted by stories he had heard from European friends, and Coyoacán looked just like the promising place he had been imagining. This was to be his new paradise, a place to earn a good living, and a haven from his father's second marriage and a rather unfriendly stepmother. He left home as a teenager by the usual means in those days—an ocean liner. Shortly after his ship arrived at the port of Veracruz on the Gulf of Mexico, nineteen-year-old Wilhelm made his way to Mexico City. Like so many immigrants, the modern capital enticed him to be part of it. Although more and more people were migrating there in search of work, no one seemed to look anywhere else. As the son of a painter and goldsmith, and trained in both the art of jewelry and photography, Wilhelm soon began working at these trades. It was not always easy to feel like part of the new society in which he had landed, however. First, he had to learn Spanish and then he had to get to know people. Since his foreign-sounding name made him an outsider in his new homeland, Wilhelm quickly changed his name to the Spanish equivalent—Guillermo—and became a naturalized citizen.

In Mexico City, Guillermo met María Cerdeña who worked at the same store, and they married three years later. Their first child, a daughter, represented the opening chapter to what promised to be a happy family story. The birth of their second daughter, however, involved all sorts of medical complications. The baby survived but, sadly, María Cerdeña died very shortly after. A young father left alone, Guillermo was distraught: he had only spent three years in this new country, and these had been filled with the companionship of a wife and growing family. Left with two orphaned daughters, and feeling abandoned, he did not wait long to remarry. One of his associates at *La Perla* (The Pearl), the same Mexico City jewelry store where he had worked since his arrival from Germany, caught his eye.

Guillermo Kahlo had opened a fledgling photographic studio above the store, and had started to make a reputation in that field. Photography was enjoying popularity as a new form of art, and Guillermo was talented at capturing scenes and portraits. He would later tell his family that he preferred photographing buildings to people, but in the beginning he worked from this small studio above the store and did portraits of parents and children. His new work companion, Matilde Calderón y González, was the daughter of a woman from Oaxaca and a military father. Another recent arrival in Mexico City, Matilde noticed Guillermo's dedication to both professions, and his general seriousness. She had been brought up strictly, according to tradition, in the Catholic Church and she would not have been interested in anything other than a formal relationship with the young man. Four short months after the death of María Cerdeña, Guillermo and Matilde married, on February 21, 1898. All records show that theirs was not a passionate relationship; rather, their marriage was the formalizing of a friendship. A lonely man, or a nostalgic man, or a melancholy man—three of the judgments that were most commonly offered about Guillermo by Frida and her sisters—he did not last long as a widower. Their union produced five children—four daughters and a son who died very young—including the future artist and celebrity Frida in 1907. So, Coyoacán was to be the place for another new beginning; Matilde and the girls represented the second part of Guillermo's life. And the *Casa Azul*—the dramatic Blue House—that he built for them all is a symbol of the hope that Frida would inherit.

Matilde, Adriana, Frida, and Cristina were the daughters of Guillermo and Matilde, girls photographed often by their father, even though he claimed to dislike taking pictures of people because the other subject of his work—monuments—was much easier to capture in print. His daughters would have their pictures taken, though, especially when their father was at home with them. Photos of Frida taken before she turned two show a small, round-faced, smiling girl with dark eyes, dressed in the voluminous blouses and numerous ribbons that a traditional Mexican family would have selected to make their children look presentable in formal photographs. Both the poses and the clothing were conventions of the times. When couples posed for a portrait, the woman would be standing behind the man, possibly resting her hand on his arm, but having no other physical contact. Both would face forward, looking at the camera or beyond it, and remain composed. A child would be seated formally on a chair, motionless and calm. What they would be wearing did not vary—a dark suit for him, a long dress for her, something starched and formal for the child.

So, this image of Frida presents a typical kind of portrait down to the last detail. Even with a dark and fairly mysterious sepia background, the young Frida's pudgy cheeks, dancing eyes, and mischievous grin give a glimpse of the energy she struggled to keep under control as she sat still for the photographer (her father), hands obediently folded on her lap. She does not always face us directly, but sometimes sits at a slight angle, with her head tilted a bit so that her eyes look at us but not straight on and her legs are folded to one side, tucked underneath her. How long would she have had to remain quiet until the picture was taken? More than a few minutes were needed with the photographic processes of the time, and one can almost imagine *la niña Frida*—little Frida, a term of affection used first by her family and later by Diego—running off as soon as the session was over. In the early 1900s, there were only two kinds of photographs of children: a child was captured either as an eager imp, frozen in time for a few minutes like Frida while the chemicals and light did their work; or a still body, the dead child's last portrait. Full of life, Frida was probably an impatient child, even as she dutifully smiled for the camera. Then she might have disappeared into the garden. This photo was a celebration, not a commemoration.

A later photo of her at four, this time showing her from head to toe, confirms that the chubby, impish little girl with a bouquet of flowers, was just waiting to slide off the wooden bench and rush out of the room. But photographs at the time were studio affairs, sessions with certain fixed positions and backdrops that were the signs of official portraits. It seems most likely that her father enticed her to sit for him in the Blue House, since an excursion to his city studio would entail lots of planning and travel. Even at home, however, he would have arranged an acceptable pose for her. Frida's typical light-colored dress, neatly combed pageboy, and laced leather boots were not just stylish but the traditional look for her social class. Neither extremely wealthy nor part of the poor classes, she looks neat and clean and happy. To one side, we catch a glimpse of the stone wall and flower pots that lined the Blue House's terrace, leading to the greenhouse, where the window panes were made of scavenged photographic plates from Guillermo's studio. Once again, this looks like a girl poised to fly into the garden and get into mischief with her sisters, with Cristina in particular, who was only one year younger than Frida.

Traditional Mexican families of the time usually had numerous children, and the Kahlo-Calderón household was no exception. This meant that there were always siblings around to join in activities, and that rivalries and competition were just part of the regular daily routine. Not a family given to a lot of physical activity, the girls nevertheless spent a childhood with others in nearby parks and yards. Frida and Cristina were a good example of this camaraderie, starting from their first years together at home and extending through their strained relationship during Frida's marriage to painter Diego Rivera. Guillermo took photographs of Matilde, Frida, and Cristina as young women in the 1920s, in formal dress in the garden of their home. But as time went by, there were more photos of the adult Frida accompanied by other women—artists, friends, and in her last years nurses—than there were of Frida and Cristina together. In one well-known picture of Frida with her mother, sisters, cousins, and grandparents, Frida and Cristina look very different. Cristina is shown seated on a tapestry rug, with a modern, form-fitting dress and fancy shoes, her legs demurely off to one side. She is dressed as might be expected of a young woman, while Frida stands to one side, wearing a man's suit. One hand in her trouser pocket, her hair slicked down, and with a carefully knotted tie under a light colored vest, Frida has her arm resting on her grandfather's shoulder. She strikes the pose of the man in a typical portrait, standing at the side of the family over which he has control. No one appears surprised by her outfit, and their faces show either no reaction to her dress and attitude or just polite smiles. The entries in Frida's diary from the 1940s show how her distance from Cristina grew after she discovered her sister's affair with Diego. Frida also wrote of her own feeling of exclusion from the social circles in which Cristina was involved, concluding that she would never be as pretty or as popular as her younger sister. Perhaps the man's suit was a visible sign of her difference from the rest of the family around her, even at this young age. Or maybe she was looking for a way to call attention to herself in deviating from a more accepted clothing style and demeanor.

Frida later added another piece to the stories of her childhood, and opened the door into her imagination. She wrote that as a girl she would breathe warm air onto the windows of her room in the Blue House, then draw little circles onto the panes of glass frosted with the morning chill. Calling them windows into the world of imaginary friends, she thought of herself stepping through these openings and taking part in adventures outside her everyday life. These dream friends were her escape from the limits of Coyoacán and the Blue House, even if the house and its surroundings were perfect for a young girl's early years. Conforming less to society's demands than Cristina did, Frida found that life for women such as her mother was too limiting. Spending all of her time in the house caring for her daughters, Matilde Calderón seemed to have lost the passion for life that Frida cultivated in herself (Zamora 1987, 21). Church and religious activities were not how she wanted to occupy her time, and Frida began to look outside her family circle for something more. A space had opened up between Frida and her mother, one that the young girl filled with a self-sufficient attitude way beyond her years. In turn, her mother sensed that she did not need to pay this daughter as much attention and turned toward the others instead. The house was full of women—Matilde, the four girls, various aunts, and other friends and relatives—but Frida recalled the feeling that she was always looking beyond the walls of home for something less ordinary, and maybe even *someone* very different from the immediate family.

In her 1936 painting *My Grandparents, My Parents, and I (Family Tree)*, Frida represented herself as the product of several generations and several cultures. She placed herself as a young girl inside the walls of the Blue House—the color on the walls gives it away—situated in a Mexican geography of cactuses on one side and the narrow streets of Coyoacán on the other. Her genealogical tree is held together with a floating red ribbon that she holds in one hand and that reaches up to the two generations of formal-looking grandparents surrounding Guillermo and Matilde. The German Jews from Baden-Baden on the right, the photographer from Morelia and his Oaxacan wife on the left, float above a painted version of her parents' wedding photograph that was in their home and is now in the Blue House museum. Frida looks just like the plump little girl with dark hair in the photos her father took of her when she was still under 4 years old, but the other two generations share the stiffness and formality of official adult portraits. Europe and America, Germany and Mexico, cross the landscape, unite her parents, and produce Frida herself. The center of her world, the Blue House and Coyoacán, compose the terrain on which she has found her footing (she is painted naked with no clothing around her at all and no shoes), her bare feet in direct contact with the earth. The elders are demurely clothed and elegantly dressed for their painted portraits; Frida is part of a natural world—and of a Mexico—that holds them all together. What might she have inherited from these family members and the mixture of cultures? This is a question she dealt with in her art over the course of her life.

There were certainly new and often unexpected events happening all around the family as Frida grew up, but usually at something of a distance. The relative peace of Coyoacán was a stark contrast to the political and social clashes across northern Mexico, and in almost every other city regardless of size. Pancho Villa, Emiliano Zapata, and their troops came and went on horseback and on the railroads, crisscrossing the country as they fought over competing visions for the future of Mexico and disputed divisions of power. It was both a war of social classes and of political ideas as governments came and went, leaving a trail of blood and dust in their wake. No one wanted to give in to the enemy because it would mean that all their supporters would lose as well, and there would be a fight to the death. These national events filled the nation with both hope and fear, and filled families with stories of survival and disappearance.

As the Mexican Revolution came galloping into Mexico City in the shape of Pancho Villa and his soldiers, Frida and her family in Coyoacán were isolated from any direct contact with the struggle, yet everyone talked about it. Visitors to the city returned to Coyoacán to pass along real information, tall tales, and even romantic legends about the captivating eyes of the young soldiers who rode into small towns and swept girls off their feet and into the sunset, never to be seen again. Politics and love came together in the *corridos*—catchy popular songs of heroes and villains—that Frida and her sisters learned by heart. Frida told friends that she and her sisters locked themselves in a closet in the Blue House to sing choruses of revolutionary songs in support of the rebels, but this formed part of her memories (or inventions) when she was grown up. The extent of the direct effect of the 1910 Revolution on the Kahlo-Calderón family was, then, more in relation to the music that showed their private sympathy for the cause than direct political activism. Is her remembrance of these scenes fact or fiction? Perhaps it involves a bit of both, but it gives us a lovely image of a family of women enticed by the stories of events swirling around them in exciting revolutionary times. Later on, Frida would embellish her childhood again by changing her date of birth from 1907, a date with less romance, to 1910, the year the Revolution began. In doing so, Frida became a daughter of radical change. When asked, she could identify herself with a momentous event of which she claimed to form a part. Frida and the monumental Mexican Revolution would share a dramatic beginning.

The real effect of the Mexican Revolution on the family was economic. Always a hard worker, the changing times would threaten Guillermo's businesses with the loss of sales and clientele. Frida's niece Isolda remembers that Guillermo had his ups and downs in the photography studio over the decade that began in 1910, since the country on the verge of revolution and then in the midst of fighting affected the fortunes of many. Not every family would have the money for photographs, and a government in dispute would not hire a photographer of monuments with a war going on. Jewelry was also not a necessity in times of struggle. As a result, Guillermo ended up having to take loans out against the Blue House to keep the family afloat. This is much easier to corroborate with receipts and bills than the chorus of women in the darkness of the closet, but it also shows less sentimentality and passion—two of Frida's greatest assets as a storyteller. Guillermo's solitary nature compounded his sadness over such problems, and he would soon have to cope with another situation in the family that would take all of his energy.

Frida recounted her first few years in Coyoacán as a normal, if secluded, period of time, punctuated by family visits and other routine events. But the normality ended when she was stricken by polio at the age of six.

A child of physical activity and full of the spark of life, Frida lost the strength in one leg to this disease. One of the scourges of the early twentieth century, polio epidemics swept across Mexico City as they did New York City and the towns and villages of many other countries around the world. The disease left the young Frida with her first physical challenge: a thin and wasted leg that she would try to hide in every photo taken of her from then on. She tucked it behind her healthy leg, or covered it with white opaque stockings, or wore long skirts, or even got men's overalls so that the pants would hide her skinny leg. Always jealous of Cristina, thinking her more attractive and popular, Frida was self-conscious of her flaw. Although her father's remedy was to get her out walking or riding a bicycle every day, she began to worry about what people would think of her. And she began to look out at the world with more and more defiance, especially at the world outside Coyoacán.

On her street in Coyoacán, then later when she attended the local German school at her father's insistence, she got the nickname *Pata de Palo* (Peg Leg) from her playmates. Many years later, she wrote to friends and signed the letters with this almost endearing nickname. At first embarrassed by the reference to her leg, and wanting to turn her friends' and peers' interest toward her talents and not her flaws, she began to take a more defensive tone toward others and even started referring to herself by the name they gave her in order to mock it. Childish cruelty thus conditioned her to be aware of the eyes of other people looking at her; she would take this into adult life but turn it on its head as a desire to call attention to herself. What started as an insult became part of her personality, and even an endearing term when she met Diego Rivera. Never again would Frida be an innocent bystander or a naïve girl. Her life of challenges and obstacles had now begun and her health—or illnesses—would turn into the focal point of her life story. This was only the start of her turning negatives into positives as a tactic for survival, and of focusing on her body as a canvas for creating a public image that she herself tried to control.

In the years following her bout with polio, Frida emerged from Coyoacán to accompany her father as he shot photographs for the Mexican government as documents of social progress, to attend church (much too often, she said) with the many women in her extended family, and at the age of fifteen to attend high school. In the 1920s, young women in Mexico were taught to run the home, take control over the economy of the family, and become moral models so that they would find suitable men to marry. Matilde tried to make sure that her daughters fit into that scheme. One older sister had entered a convent, another had married, and younger sister Cristina seemed equally dedicated to her pursuit of a husband, with an active social life and many young suitors. With her thin leg, Frida seemed to be less of a catch. While her mother focused on Cristina, Frida turned away from social events and toward her father's profession.

And Guillermo had other ideas for Frida, anyway. She had always been the daughter with whom he shared so much, and who had spent more time with him than with any other family member. An epileptic as the result of an accident during his days in Germany, Guillermo took Frida along with him on photo assignments to help carry the heavy equipment and to care for him should he fall ill on the road. After her polio, Frida shared even more with her father than before. It was extremely unconventional for a young girl to join the ranks of boys in a college-preparatory institution, but Guillermo decided Frida's intelligence made her worthy of education. His son having died in infancy, Guillermo thought Frida was a perfect candidate to become a professional. In 1922, he helped her enroll in the model *Escuela Nacional Preparatoria* (National Preparatory School) or *Prepa*. She was just 15 and at the age when marriage would have been on the horizon. Her father had always favored her over her sisters as the child most like himself—whether in looks or in temperament is unclear, but both similarities were quite evident—so this decision had Frida take her father's place in a system he had never managed to enter. Besides, he seemed to find pleasure in contradicting his wife Matilde by choosing to send Frida for advanced education rather than grooming her to run a home and raise a family. Not only did her mother react badly to a young woman attending classes to ready herself for college, but she was also horrified to hear that the school itself was in the center of the big city. This was no longer the local German school for younger children that she had attended faithfully in Coyoacán, but a nationally recognized, first-rate place; the *Prepa* was a whole new world for Frida. Matilde was not pleased, but Frida saw this as a great opportunity to avoid her mother's type of home life. Almost instinctively bored by the limits of a maternal life, Frida was enthusiastic at the news of her taking the entrance exams for school. Perhaps Guillermo thought she could do what he had never been able to—get an advanced degree. Or maybe he just wanted to make sure Frida would always be the different daughter, the one noticed for something out of the ordinary, the one that shared his artistic and psychological temperament. They had a closer bond than Frida had with Matilde.

After the end of the Porfirio Díaz dictatorship, the elected Mexican governments had put a lot of emphasis on developing the country's educational system. Bringing it out of the nineteenth century and into modern times with new progressive proposals after the Revolution, the government ministers of education looked toward Europe for models of modern learning and to their own citizens for the raw material for building a new Mexico. If there were more advanced schools, Mexico could become a bigger player in international affairs; thus, the Ministry of Education created this particular school in Mexico City to be the very best. It was renowned as a model for all the rest to emulate. Government ministers put their pedagogical theories to the test in the *Prepa*, and to be among the first graduates was a great honor. In that atmosphere, Frida could enroll in the science courses that would teach her what she would need to pass the college entrance exams later on, and from there she could become a doctor as she had dreamed of doing. That was all well and good, and there was no better place go than the *Prepa*, but in those classes she would also get to meet many new people her own age from different backgrounds and different parts of the city, and this was certainly as much an attraction for her as the promise of an advanced education. Never content with traditions and social norms, Frida looked forward to her new challenge. In Mexico, at the *Prepa*, no one knew her and she could become whatever she wanted. Coyoacán had been a protective beginning, but the *zócalo* or enormous public square at the center of Mexico City was just like the imaginary doorway drawn on her windowpane: it opened into another social dimension. The *Prepa* was the beginning of the next stage of Frida's life.

Little did Frida know that her father's decision to send her there would change her life forever. Not only did the ratio of three hundred boys to five girls entice her (and horrify her mother), but the journey itself from small town to big city also enthralled her. And the thrill of passing the entrance exam with ease gave Frida the boost her ego needed. Nothing could stop her now! With this great opportunity at hand, Frida began to cultivate new friends and find any way she could to stand out. What was wrong with being one girl among many young men? Did her hair and clothing have a less-than-feminine look? That was fine and called attention to her. Was she hanging out with the guys and not the few other girls? Were they using street slang and answering back when girls were supposed to be demure? All of these possibilities thrilled her. Recently enrolled in the *Prepa*, Frida could make her mark on a society she found too conservative, too boring, too rigid. Coyoacán did not offer her a variety of experiences or the thrills and danger of doing things on her own. If she was unable to sit still for a photograph at the age of four, she certainly couldn't sit patiently in a class at 15 and absorb information as a passive sponge. The image of her father as an outsider in Mexico—having a foreign-sounding name, speaking Spanish with a German accent, preferring solitude—may have sparked the idea of a rebellion, but Frida worked as hard as she could to go further. In 1923, a year into her classes at the *Prepa*, Frida helped her older sister Matilde Kahlo run away to Veracruz with her boyfriend Francisco (Paco) Hernández. The woeful laments of her mother and the shocked silence of her father had little effect on Frida, since her intuition probably told her this was a good thing to have done. After all, it was her sister's decision, and it went against all social logic for a young woman. And it had been their secret as well. Running away for love was a romantic and revolutionary notion, one Frida would live by for the rest of her life. Matilde and Paco stayed together for the rest of their lives, but Frida's parents were dramatically disturbed by their rejection of the norm. Frida would always be a nonconformist, and maybe her sister Matilde was her first, perhaps unwitting, model.

The *Prepa* was an invitation to learn from cutting-edge instructors, and to become part of the intellectual ferment that would take charge of the country down the line. Several of the many male students at the *Prepa* had separated into a small group and dubbed themselves *Los Cachuchas*—the name for the caps they wore but also a slang term for people who were a bit crazy—and it was no surprise that Frida was drawn to them right away. Classes did not excite her, but loud and boisterous debate did. Not only did she like the male company, but the intellectual debates also made her feel different from the other girls, as she considered them to be trivial and childish. They were just like the sisters she had left behind in Coyoacán, and just like her mother. Why come so far to reproduce the same environment? Seven boys and two girls, the core of the group, would meet in hallways and nearby cafes to discuss philosophy and politics. Since politics were on the mind of almost everyone in a country recently out of a revolution, Frida avidly joined the group. The debating skills she learned from them—more like raucous encounters than calm discussions—would later influence her. When overwhelmed by her husband, painter Diego Rivera, and when she attended meetings of the Communist Party, whose members were also overwhelmingly male, she stood up and took the floor. She learned to hold her own in any discussion, and to initiate some of her own when she thought she was not the center of attention or being taken seriously. Even before she took on the field of art, Frida learned to express her emotions and opinions in public through the *Cachuchas*.

The undisputed leader of the *Cachuchas* was a young man by the name of Alejandro Gómez Arias, a charismatic classmate who was wonderful at public speaking. He came from a wealthy and influential family, and was on the way to becoming a lawyer, as many others in the *Prepa* planned to do (that is, if they weren't going into medicine). Frida developed a serious crush on Gómez Arias, who she saw as the antithesis of the men that courted her sisters, and represented the opposite of her father's withdrawal from the world. He was elegant, had a great sense of humor, and besides his intellectual abilities he was even a fairly good athlete. Whether Gómez Arias was her friend, or her boyfriend, isn't perfectly clear, but he called her his lifelong friend and, enigmatically, "way more than boyfriend and girlfriend" (Zamora 1987, 20), but she was much too young for anything formal at the age of 15. She found in him an openness she wasn't used to, but his family was not thrilled about the girl from Coyoacán whose family had no connections to their social circle. Although other events would break them up before the family did, his parents tried their hardest to keep them apart. In the friendship between Frida and Alejandro—or Alex as she liked to call him—they were schoolmates, members of the *Cachuchas* and, perhaps more fatefully, traveling companions to and from Coyoacán. It was on one of those trips back and forth to the *Prepa* that their close relationship and emotional ties would be sorely tested.

Another of the *Cachuchas*, Miguel N. Lira, was already in college studying Chinese poetry; he attended their café meetings as he always had even after he had graduated. A skilled writer, he would publish plays and literary journals all his life. He and Frida remained close friends as well, and he supported her by publishing positive reviews of her art. Others in the group studied law, became professors of psychiatry, or pursued a career in literature. Manuel González Ramírez defended Frida in her divorce from Diego in 1939 and remained her friend until the end. What held them together as a group was not just being students in the same school but a rejection of the solemnity of the classroom. The *Cachuchas* debated Marx and Engels, Hegel and Kant, and theories of economics and politics, but they also played practical jokes. Sometimes they cut class to hang out in the streets or debate in the hallways. They deliberately burned murals commissioned by the federal government to beautify and honor the new educational system on the walls of the *Prepa* to show that they were against all types of solemnity. It would be a mistake to call this prank an artistic judgment of the murals of painters as famous and favored as Orozco, Siqueiros, or Rivera; they just wanted to stir things up in a Mexico they thought had been all too serious for too long. Future leaders of the country and in the arts, the *Cachuchas* provoked their elders and called attention to themselves, as many young people do.

They also harassed painters like Diego Rivera, painting public murals of national heroes, standing on his scaffold high above them every day as he worked with colorful pigments on plaster. A physically unattractive man, taller than most Mexican men, with eyes that seemed to pop out of his face and a paunch that was evidence of good food and better drink, Diego was nevertheless larger-than-life and a public celebrity. His size echoed his prestige and his talent, and when Diego entered a room, everyone would stop what they were doing. He had a reputation for carrying a gun, liked to frequent *cantinas* (popular Mexican bars), and was proud of his womanizing. He would be an easy target for the students in the *Prepa,* and to get him to pay attention to them, the *Cachuchas* soaped his ladder so he would fall or threw firecrackers down the hall. Bored, Frida frequently cut classes, but when she saw this giant of a man on the scaffold, she found a new and better reason to attend school. If Alex was her intellectual challenge, Diego became her emotional challenge. Closer in age to her father, Diego Rivera would certainly be a perfect player in an adolescent's rebellion. He was 36, she was 15; he was married, she lived at home with her parents; he was large and serenely sure of himself, she was tiny and impetuous. From day one, Frida announced to everyone that she was going to marry Diego Rivera.

Was this a provocation or a wish? Carlos Fuentes says that Frida attended the *Prepa* when modern Mexico was emerging to discover "the indiscreet, if liberating, charms of intuition, children, Indians" (2005, 10). Small, strident, definitely imprudent and indiscreet but totally guileless, Frida was part of this process of liberation. Youth was crucial in this age of discovery, with a young nation and a young woman both finding ways of expressing their intuition (of dreams and fantasies) and their childlike innocence. For Frida, there was freedom from familial restraints and doors closed to different opinions; for the country, a door was opening to the world of the imagination, and it was inventing itself in a new form after the Revolution. The stage was set for another revolutionary moment for them both.

In this heady environment, Frida lived each day to the fullest. Taunting Rivera at every turn, she also spent most of her days in the company of Gómez Arias. Frida saw the coldness between her parents—her mother told her that before Guillermo there had been another young man who had committed suicide before they married, and that she never found real love with her husband (Zamora 1987, 20)—and found an antidote for it in these two men. Whether it was because of the differences between her and Diego or because she detected a chance to shake her family up, Frida often mentioned her feelings of love at first sight for him. Diego was living with one woman—Lupe Marín—but having affairs with others at the same time. This was just the ammunition Frida needed to tease him, and she did so at every turn. She would tell him that one woman was coming when another walked in the door, or that a girlfriend had come by when he was talking to Marín. It would take seven years before she finally got him to marry her in 1929, but Frida was nothing if not persistent. Through Diego, Frida would discover politics at the personal level as well as on an international stage. She would also continue to learn how to create myths about herself and to fabricate stories that made an audience stop and listen. Learning from Diego's egocentric behavior, and his inability to be faithful, Frida outdid him whenever she got the chance. Not needing too much coaching given her imaginary childhood friends, Frida added to these basic instincts and grew into a recognizable public figure not only at ease with being looked at, but also demanding her share of attention. She could tell as tall a tale as Diego could, and was able to shock prim society in many ways. Less than one half the size of Diego Rivera, Frida Kahlo had to do something to keep from disappearing. When interviewed about their unequal size but growing equality of artistic talent, Frida responded that she had to be like a dot of green in a sea of red paint.

But as she courted Diego in her own peculiar way, stories of other romances and emotional complications arose. In 1925, Frida wrote a letter to Gómez Arias signaling that their relationship had ended—the cause of this is not clear—and underlining how sad this made her. His family had tried all possible ways to separate them, including sending him to Europe and taking him far away during breaks from school. Whether the cause came from them or from her own interest in too many other people, August of 1925 marked a change between Frida and Alex. A certain detachment from emotional relationships haunted Frida the rest of her life, even as she touted her oneness with Diego or her intimacy with other artists and photographers like Nikolas Muray or Isamu Noguchi. Something between Alex and Frida produced a permanent sense of vulnerability and remoteness in her. The next month, on September 17, 1925, a definitive rupture occurred that simultaneously broke apart any romance, her health, and her future at the *Prepa*. Just as traditional ideas and modern changes coexisted in Mexico in the 1920s, old and new modes of transportation were also seen side-by-side. Frida and Alex were used to taking the bus from Coyoacán to the doorstep of the *Prepa*, and then returning home the same way. The buses ran along the broad new avenues, planned as boulevards of a great city that would rival any European capital; they were marvels of engineering and, for that time, speed and efficiency. Made of wooden frames bent like the hull of a ship, the buses connected places like Coyoacán with downtown Mexico City and gave people access to schools, stores, and markets all over the region. Instead of models of small-town isolation, travelers to the city were becoming models of everyday mobility on these vehicles.

There are many different claims about the exact place and time of the incident, but the element these versions have in common is the catastrophic nature of the bus accident in which Frida was involved. After spending the previous two days coming and going from the annual independence celebrations of September 15 and 16, 1925, Frida and Alex left the *Prepa* on the afternoon of the 17th to return to Coyoacán on the bus. On the way, they passed by stands set up along the side of the avenue to sell toys and trinkets to the noisy celebrants. Unsuccessful in her quest to replace a parasol she had lost, Frida settled for a wooden toy and they boarded the bus. Shortly after it left the stop, the driver—a novice at the wheel of the new machine—tried to pass a slow-moving trolley that was maneuvering around a corner. The move didn't work, and the bus crashed against the other vehicle, breaking into hundreds of wooden fragments. Alex fared better than Frida. His clothing had been ripped apart and he had lost hold of the toy he was carrying for her. But as he looked over the pile of rubble at the crash site, he didn't see her. Then he spotted her, naked and bloody, lying on the ground. Her clothing had been completely torn off and the handrail of the bus had gone straight through her, piercing her stomach and pelvis. The tube of metal entered on one side of her and was sticking out the other side. As if this wasn't horrifying enough, the gold dust that another passenger had been carrying home in a vial covered her from head to foot, stuck in the blood she was losing. A worker dressed in overalls, a good Samaritan, decided it was best to pull the metal handrail out and he did so with Frida screaming the entire time. He just put his foot on her and heaved on the piece of metal until it came out of her body. As they waited for an ambulance, and with all of the passengers in shock over the gravity of what had seemed a slow-motion collision, Alex covered Frida with what was left of his coat. When the Red Cross and medical personnel began to divide the wounded into categories, they placed Frida among the untreatable. It took Alex some time to get them to agree that she needed attention; if not for him, Frida would most likely have died then and there. In fact, there was some debate in the newspapers over whether she actually survived.

This does not mean that Frida recovered from this terrible accident, whether in physical or mental terms, since recovery would indicate that she could leave it behind. Her years of treatment, the search for new ways to deal with the pain, and her numerous surgical operations all stem from this. But her turn from medicine to art was also a result of this fateful day in September. The content of her paintings and the detailed studies of her own face and body—some of the most recognizable aspects of Kahlo's self-portraits and sketches and her uniqueness in women's art—are the productive outcome of her trauma. She spent a month at the Red Cross and then several years recovering at home in Coyoacán. With numerous broken ribs, cervical fractures in her spine, and a leg broken in 11 places,

Frida would need a lot of care. In the 1920s, this would of course be limited, but she got the care available. If real physical and psychological healing was possible, that was more of a relative question. The next day, the Mexico City newspaper *Excélsior* reported on the severity of the accident and noted that she might be among the passengers that had since died in the Red Cross hospital. While she obviously did survive, Frida would never return to the *Prepa;* she had to leave her friends, and ended up developing her talent as an artist during her long, long confinement at home. Almost entombed in a body cast, Frida invented a system of pulleys and ropes for her canopied bed that kept her as motionless as she was supposed to be but allowed for some tiny movement of her arm and hand. Then, she had mirrors installed above her on the canopy. And so, in symbolic terms, Frida Kahlo the artist was born, and Frida Kahlo the future doctor died.

Almost a year to the day after the accident, Frida drew a sketch of what she remembered. Partly a dream sequence because she had been unconscious most of the time, and partly therapy, this small pencil drawing shows what she recalled of the chaos of the moment. On the top half of the page is the literal encounter of the bus and the trolley, with one embedded in the side of the other. There are bodies scattered on the ground everywhere, and people hanging out of the windows of both vehicles. Some forms are flattened by the impact and lie near or under the bus; others are sitting with head in hands, stunned and motionless. Frida gave the bus 12 wheels, a highly improbable fact, but maybe a metaphor for the overwhelming feeling of being crushed by something enormous and powerful. All of these wheels are raised in the air, not touching the ground. Somewhere between the heavy wooden frame and a strange weightlessness lie the victims suspended in disbelief. The dream of modern transportation has turned into a nightmare for the passengers.

On the bottom half of the page, Frida sketched a building with barred windows, a bandaged body on a stretcher and, right in the center, a close-up of a young woman with short dark hair and thick eyebrows. On closer inspection, it is obviously a self-portrait of Frida. She portrays herself in full view as a wounded and bandaged person and then in smaller portrait form as a victim with a face. The handles of the stretcher have the words *Cruz Roja* (Red Cross) lettered on them, and all of these images connect across the space of the page as a collage of sentiments and emotions rather than historical facts. An accident, a medical rescue, and a small survivor come together almost on top of each other to form a singular moment in Frida's life. Lasting a few minutes in real time, the effects of the accident will last a lifetime. Frida was only 18 years old.

Chapter 2

"MY TWO ACCIDENTS"

The general collapse of Frida's health, the end of her daily contact with her friends the *Cachuchas*, and the demise of her future medical career all occurred with the bus crash on the afternoon of September 17, 1925. There are several versions of the exact medical results of the accident, but all inevitably lead to the same conclusion: after a month in the hospital, Frida returned to Coyoacán and the beloved Blue House to spend the next two years of her life recuperating. Both her physical and mental health suffered, with depression circling around her as she envisioned death as a skeleton that visited her bedroom each evening. With frequent ups and downs, alternating between healing and setbacks, Frida was spending her days far away from the *Prepa* and from Gómez Arias. As an adolescent, barely into her last teenaged year, Frida became estranged from one of the most critical aspects of life at that age: social activity. Her body might heal, and she could overcome mental anguish with time, but the lack of social contact left a deep mark. She and Gómez Arias stayed in touch by letter, but with the entire city between them and their families keeping them at a distance, it seemed as if an ocean separated them. Gómez Arias—the "dear Alex" or "my darling Alex" of her letters, all of which he kept—answered most if not all of her notes and commented on her drawings when she sent them. Frida repeatedly complained of being desperately bored, strapped into an endless variety of corsets and pulleys, and devices that put her into a kind of suspended animation. She had to get used to seeing the world from a prone position, not eye-to-eye. She often became depressed, seeing no end to doctors' visits and provisional therapies. And she saw less and less of Alex. Even though they had broken off their more intimate social contact before the accident, Frida wrote to him with an urgent tone, often trying to reconcile whatever differences had separated them. He inhabited a world of open doors and she lived in a closed-off room.

Then there was the home front. Adding the need to pay her medical bills to the family's mounting financial problems, Frida's accident also compounded personal tensions among family members. Her parents had never been passionately close, and this event drove a greater wedge between them. Frida's mother Matilde would suffer bouts of depression too, and her desperation provoked epileptic seizures like the ones her husband Guillermo had suffered from for years. This did not help the atmosphere when Frida returned home from the Red Cross Hospital, since there was no one calm enough to ease the fears of the patient and her family. Frida was trapped inside four walls that seemed like a jail, and her mother's increasingly delicate condition limited her ability to support her fragile daughter. In a panic over whether her wounds would heal, being pulled in by the hysteria around her, and not wanting to lose Gómez Arias totally, Frida wrote and wrote, flooding her friend Alex with mail. The language of these letters grew more and more strident and fearful: she referred to the medical treatments as her "martyrdom" (Zamora 1987, 26–27), to the proposal of using heat and bone grafts as torture, and gave him horrifyingly exact details of her daily routine. One of the most frightful passages is Frida's description of the plaster cast from her neck to her legs that had to dry as she was suspended from the ceiling by a winch. For two and a half hours, with her toes barely touching the ground, Frida waited for the relief (if that was what it really was) of getting back into bed, lying flat on her back in a perfectly rigid position for the next few months. Immobile, Frida began the lifelong process of self-analysis that she would continue in her self-portraits during these lonely periods of isolation. Her body becomes her focus, and through it she perceived everything and everyone around her.

After the first rounds of treatment for her wounds and the fractures of her pelvis and abdominal cavity, doctors found a spinal problem most likely unrelated to the traffic accident but now revealed in diagnostic x-rays: congenital scoliosis. A collection of symptoms including many types of malformation of the natural curvature of the spine, today scoliosis is treatable with more modern forms of braces or with surgical intervention. In the 1920s, Frida had fewer options. Actually, scoliosis added to the physical complications of the accident rather than causing problems on its own. With a weakened skeletal structure and numerous broken and shattered bones, the last thing Frida needed was for her body to exhibit another abnormality. Perhaps the exaggerated curvature of her spinal column—which she later painted frequently in her self-portraits as the shattered foundation for her entire skeletal structure—prolonged Frida's immobility, since her body needed a longer time to heal. It also revealed a physical weakness that would increase with age and add to the difficulty of walking and generally getting around later in life. In addition to being a physical challenge, Frida's spine—the basic support of the architecture of the human body—became a vivid image which she sketched and painted, peeling back layers of skin to show the crumbling bones on which her visible body rested.

When she began to use paints and plaster boards as the durable surfaces for her artwork, though, Frida did not immediately turn to the symbol of the broken spinal column, but instead to a soft, rather sweet self-portrait style. She was still a young woman after all, not mature in experience or expertise, and she was desperately interested in creating a likeness of herself that could stand in for her with Gómez Arias and accompany him day and night. Frida could not be with him during her convalescence, and so she used a stand-in: her self-portrait. From her remote part of the city, the painting was a cry for attention; from his perspective, it showed a figure from the past. By late 1926, a year after the accident, Frida questioned why he studied so much and she turned to art as a new mode of expression to replace classes and the *Prepa*. They had been in the accident together, but now little connected the two of them. They no longer took classes together and they did not meet to debate hot issues. Alex was moving toward his goal of practicing law; Frida was not moving at all. She had literally been frozen in her tracks, at least in terms of her education and her social connections. Not waiting for life to pass him by, and encouraged by his family, Gómez Arias pursued his interest in the law and embarked on a European adventure as a rite of passage into the adult world. Young men of means in Mexico would make such voyages to the motherland (Spain) or to the capitals of culture such as Paris or Rome. As Frida spent much of 1926 and 1927in bed in Coyoacán, Gómez Arias traveled the world. Frida continued writing, sending him boxes and boxes of letters even as he traveled abroad, making sure that he did not forget her. However, things between them would never be the same.

At home, Frida was fitted for new corsets and tried new treatments; she deserted her studies once and for all and told Gómez Arias that he was lucky to have seen with his own eyes all of the architectural structures and famous paintings they had read about in their books at the *Prepa*. Her tone was both nostalgic for what she had lost and desperately angry over her exclusion from so many activities. Frida was not patient with her condition, and she envied the young women around her who grew up and got married and became part of a world she looked at only from her room. There was no comparison between the two types of life. Despite Guillermo's promises to take her to Veracruz when she was well enough to travel, to show her the port where he had first arrived from Germany, Frida knew that it would be difficult for her father to fulfill this promise when his own health was not strong. Besides, Veracruz was not Europe and Guillermo was not Alex. Alex wrote to Frida that the Mediterranean was as blue as the pictures in their textbooks; she wondered whether she would ever see it with her own eyes. Her parents blamed the accident on her independent spirit and carelessness. It was not her ill health, but rather her bad choices and unpredictable temperament that kept them from allowing her to return to the *Prepa.* The chapter of her life there, brief as it was, had ended.

In 1928, Frida painted an oil portrait of Gómez Arias which she dedicated to him 30 years later. In the upper right hand corner, she wrote: "Alex—with affection I painted this portrait of you as my comrade, as always, Frida." It is a simple painting of a serious young man dressed in a suit and tie, unsmiling and serene, on a flat red background. He stares out, as Frida does in her self-portraits, calmly looking at the world with all the hopes of youth in his eyes. This painting could almost be called a companion piece to the 1926 self-portrait that she sent to Gómez Arias so that he could always remember what she looked like. The paintings are of similar size and both faces are serene and steady. As a photograph would accompany a dear friend or a family member today, this painting was meant to be a remembrance, a face frozen in time. She asked Gómez Arias to put it at eye level so they could carry on an imaginary conversation eye-to-eye. Frida did not want him to think of her as an invalid, prostrate and helpless.

Dedicating the image to him, and signing it from "your Botticelli," Frida swirled waves across the dark background and has her likeness place one hand across her waist, the elongated fingers looking long and tapered and extended far out to the side. The hands mimic the waves in their soft bends and curves. The darkness behind her is reminiscent of a storm and not the turquoise, stylized waves of Botticelli's *Venus* emerging from the sea on a clamshell, evoked by the reference to the Italian artist. The pink roses, and the sprites or nymphs blowing air across Botticelli's scene, barely rippling Venus's golden cloth, have been replaced by a somber ocean cast in tones of deep red. There is nothing bright or pleasant about this seaside scene; everything is dark and gloomy. It is hard to avoid associating this melancholy tone with the accident, and the red with Frida's own blood. Both were fresh in her mind. Frida also painted herself in red brocade, the deep neck of her garment elongating her neck even further and contrasting with her pale skin. She looks frail and white, not full of life. Only 19 years old when she painted this for her friend Alex in 1926, Frida was slim, delicate, and elegant. Her hair is pulled taut and she does not smile. A cleft chin like her father's is visible, linking her to the family that surrounds her as she recovers, but creating even more tension in her development as a young woman in a modern world, since they stand in her way of returning to it. Maybe the chin tilts up a bit, defying the world around her, but Frida appears alone and solemn. Her signature winged eyebrows are evident in this early painting, above clear brown eyes that seem too steady in their gaze ever to blink. The painted Frida is beautiful, tormented, and she seems to be daring Gómez Arias to just try and forget her. In Spanish, torment and storm—*tormento and tormenta*—are words that only differ by one letter, so Frida's stormy waves and tortured memories come together in the painting both in the background and in her falsely impassive face. Under the surface of the water and the surface of her body there raged a real tempest.

As she recuperated during 1926 and 1927, Frida also painted portraits of her neighbor Alicia Galant, her sister Adriana, her *Prepa* friend Miguel N. Lira, a family maid, local *cantinas* with their crowds of boisterous drinkers (painted from memory while bedridden), her younger sister Cristina, and herself (over and over). Days were painfully long and the visits of friends were less and less frequent; she filled her time with art on board, on canvas, on metal, on paper. During this time, Frida made a switch from the medical drawings as she had been doing in school to personal, intimate paintings of friends and family. Her artistic talent, undeveloped until after the accident, gave Frida a new identity and a visible way to show her thoughts and feelings. Maybe it kept her from even greater isolation and despair. It also opened a new world—the art world—to her when she ventured out of the Blue House and into the studios and workshops of Diego Rivera and other artists. If the wounded young woman had been a promising doctor, she now emerged as a promising artist. She only needed some public opinion in her favor to begin working on her own myth.

In some self-portraits of a slightly later date, sometime between 1929 and 1930, Frida appeared dressed in a simple white or gray blouse, sometimes accompanied by a necklace of greenish jade beads, but always with dangling earrings. As the years passed, these would become a trademark part of her look, and would connect her with the indigenous, sometimes even pre-Columbian, world of Mexican culture. As Mexicans recovered a pride in their heritage after the years of revolutionary struggle, this became increasingly evident in the clothing, jewelry, and artwork of avant-garde intellectuals. They were proud to be seen as a part of a new Mexico that had not lost touch with its past, but rather that celebrated it by recovering the "look" of pre-Columbian art. If this sounds like a conscious decision to take on a certain style, for the most part it was. Frida stood at the forefront of the public display of Aztec, Mayan, and more contemporary crafts, now woven into cloth and garments or hanging around her neck in beaded necklaces. Her close association with Diego Rivera, also a product of her time of recuperation, influenced her as well since he was a longtime collector of artifacts and artwork. Anahuacalli, one of his later private homes, was purposely designed and built as a pyramid, filled with statues, beadwork, engravings, and many other pre-Columbian items on display. His collection was monumental in scale; Frida's link to these cultures took the form of personal adornment. Her mother was from Oaxaca, a center of indigenous art and culture, but Frida only turned toward pre-Columbian styles and themes after meeting Diego. They seemed to connect her to him and to a Mexican history in vogue during those years after the Revolution, when national identity was increasingly seen in terms of native groups in addition to the influence of Europe.

In *Self-Portrait with Airplane and Clock* (1929), Frida painted herself in front of a large balcony window through which we see a Piper Cub ascending into the heavens, framed by lush dark velvet drapes. Next to Frida is a stack of books, thick and bound in leather, and on top of them sits an alarm clock poised at 8 minutes to three. Her blushing cheeks, long neck, and single brow are unmistakable, and the lace details on the dress's cap sleeves emphasize the careful observation needed to reproduce this scene. Even if invented in her imagination or merely recollected from a previous moment, the wings of the plane and the hands on the clock fill the portrait with a hint of her powers of observation. Long periods in bed had made her aware of every tiny aspect of her environment. Immobility kept her from getting out into the world, but not from observing the nuances of things around her. The 1930 works *Self-Portrait in a Chair* and *Hand* show equal dedication to meticulous detail and shading, down to the lines on Frida's cuticles and the tiny flecks of light reflected in her brown eyes.

As Gómez Arias and the *Cachuchas* became less and less a part of her daily life, and as she developed her latent artistic talents, Frida's life took yet another turn. They had met before during her early months at the *Prepa*, when she had seen him painting frescoes on the walls before the fateful accident, but Frida re-encountered Diego Rivera as she ventured out into the social world of Coyoacán nearby. While he didn't live there,

Rivera had friends in that increasingly affluent suburb. He didn't burst into her life, as some have thought, but instead reappeared at a time when each of them was experiencing change: he was always on the prowl for women and she was anxious to get out of the house and back into the stream of daily life. Perhaps they reconnected at the popular gatherings given by Tina Modotti—artist, model, actress, political activist and companion of photographer Edward Weston—at her home, or perhaps they became involved after she brought him some of her artwork for approval. Both scenarios offered her a chance to resume at least some of her former activities, this time with a larger-than-life figure and not a young friend and student like Gómez Arias had been.

Part of a crowd of talented intellectuals and no less talented troublemakers, Rivera was both physically and socially outstanding. Rivera carried a pistol and, in bouts of drunken partying, was known to shoot into the heavens to make a point in an argument or as the punch line of a joke. He lived to provoke reactions, and found many ways to do just that. David Alfaro Siqueiros, José Clemente Orozco, and Diego Rivera were the holy trinity of official artists of the Revolution and each practiced politics, socializing, and creativity with equal intensity. Public artists were also public figures, and when Frida joined the crowd with Modotti, Weston, and Rivera, she could not sit on the sidelines and be invisible. Life would become a daily challenge for the spotlight and for attention. When Diego looked at her self-portraits and told her of their originality and her talent with paint, he opened the door to her artistic career and her future as a very public figure. But Frida found what she was looking for personally as well: someone way beyond the realm of the ordinary, everyday life of her family and her neighborhood, and someone who could help her take the first step on the road to fame. Frida began to venture into a more bohemian world of artists, galleries, and wealthy sponsors, and she started to cultivate a look that would associate her with this. Frida had always dressed as she pleased, and in ways she thought might outrage traditional society. At Rivera's side, she could use this as a weapon to incite public reaction and link her with his group of artists and provocateurs.

As difficult, complicated, and talented a personality as Frida, Diego both fascinated and terrified her. She was a tiny woman; he was a large middle-aged man. He was loud and carried a gun; bragged about his conquests of many women; drank to excess and was a member of the Communist Party. Who else could Frida look to for advice about the art she had been working on in her convalescence than Diego Rivera? She might have met other artists in Coyoacán, but she chose him. He symbolized everything she respected: being different, standing out, challenging society.

The attractive women he used as models—Nahui Ollin, Lupe Rivas Cacho, Palma Guillén—had brought the young men of the *Prepa* running to pay attention to them and to the famous Rivera as he worked inside the walls of their school. Frida, on the other hand, had often called him down from his scaffold in the Ministry of Education to tell him tall tales and jokes, interrupting his work and calling attention to herself. If crowds had been looking at Diego, she could turn their eyes toward herself by appearing at his side at all hours of the day and night. His wife at the time, Lupe Marín, was often the butt of some of Frida's jokes, and didn't find them funny. Carrying the baby Lupe, her first daughter with Rivera and, later, Ruth, their second, Marín visited his worksite frequently and did not look forward to finding the annoying young woman Frida Kahlo there. Rivera was, as always, flattered by the attention of any woman, and Frida was young at that. Unlike the admirers usually present at his parties, he didn't know her and had no idea what family she belonged to. He descended slowly from the wooden platform and engaged her in witty exchanges, creating both a scene and a bond between them. A connection was made, and it would be hard to turn back. In a 1951 interview with a newspaper reporter, Frida recalled her budding relationship with Rivera as an event as fateful as the traffic accident that caused her so much pain. By that time, quite aware of the complications of living with him, she called Diego her "second accident" (Zamora 1987, 29).

Born in 1886in Guanajuato, Rivera's talent gave him access to the prestigious Mexico City *Academia de San Carlos* (San Carlos Academy), to study fine arts at a level he could not in his hometown. There—and later in Europe—he received the best training in the traditional aspects of painting, sculpture, and drawing, imitating the styles of his teachers as well as paintings in museums. At the time, education was based on extensively copying the masters, and Rivera excelled at this. From the time he entered the academy at the tender age of ten, Rivera was a precocious child who always tried to do more. In 1907, now barely 21 years old, he won a grant to study in Spain and then in France. He spent 14 years in Paris among the avant-garde of the time, working on his art during the day and carousing in the bars at night. This bohemian life was what he later took back to Mexico, dedicating the time he did not spend painting to being a permanent fixture in Mexico City's wildest nightlife. In Paris, Rivera had spent 10 years with Angelina Beloff, a Russian artist who bore him a son, Dieguito (little Diego). The poor child died of meningitis in the freezing cold studio garret where Diego and Angelina lived, and Diego abandoned Angelina soon after his son's death. A second Russian woman, Maria Vorobieva-Stebelska (also called Marevna), also lived with Rivera and they had a daughter together. After this second, very tempestuous, relationship, Rivera returned to Mexico in 1921. But he returned alone, leaving Beloff waiting for him to reappear and Marevna alone to bring up a young daughter. Both women eventually emigrated, Beloff to Mexico and Marevna to England, and both lived without him. Rivera had no contact with either, except for the small amount of support he sent to Marevna for his daughter. Beloff never heard from him again, and never ceased waiting for him to return to her. Although she too lived in Mexico City and adopted Mexico as her home, they could have inhabited two different worlds. The Mexican capital was not the metropolis it is today, but it was still large enough for two people to avoid meeting each other.

In 1921, the post-Revolutionary pictorial art world in Mexico was in full swing. The government used writers and artists as the models for a new type of culture, and more traditional society sometimes closed ranks and resisted change. When a demand for social change and an eccentric character came together in the person of Diego Rivera, things could only get stirred up. Diego spent his formative years in Europe during the First World War and then the Russian Revolution; while there, he picked up painting techniques as much as radical political views. He arrived in Mexico fired up to put his mural skills to work for the *pueblo* (people) that had risen up against the federal government as the Russians had in their Revolution in 1917. He didn't take long to reach the ear of the Mexican government, especially José Vasconcelos, the Minister of Education, who found Rivera's politically oriented art perfect for his new vision of the country. Rivera was hired to portray scenes on public spaces that reflected the people who passed by every day and who had stood up to a dictator.

His first mural was for the *Preparatoria* where Frida was studying. So, an internationally renowned artist back from Europe met a country girl in the middle of a bustling city where public works were on the government agenda and where all eyes looked toward future generations like Frida's. Between 1923 and 1928, as Frida ventured from her home in Coyoacán only to return wounded, Rivera worked on over 200 mural panels and established himself as a star of socialist-inspired art, stirred by the Revolution and at the service of his beloved Mexico. Rivera traveled the country, getting re-acquainted with the color palette of the different regions, and made a triumphant return to Mexico City where he embarked on his most famous works. From waterworks to government palaces, Rivera covered walls with the heroism of the Mexican people. Painting for the masses and not for the few who attended gallery exhibits, Rivera proposed to bring artists and other workers together under the banner of a common labor union. For him, art was not a luxury but another type of human labor. More accustomed to colonial portraits of viceroys and Spanish nobles, or innocent children with angelic faces, the Mexican public didn't find Rivera's images much to their liking at first. His concepts were new and very distinctive. On the other hand, while Vasconcelos admired Rivera's talent and subject matter, he was not thrilled with his political activities. The Communist Party was not a welcome contributor in forging the new vision of Mexico. But Rivera managed to produce over 30,000 square meters (approximately 30,000 square yards) of mural art across both Mexico and the United States over the 36 years after his return from Europe. He did not take to being out of the spotlight, and added to his reputation with both words and deeds. Provoking scandal, whether in relation to his many women, different ideas about art, radical political notions, or with insults to his patrons, was Rivera's expertise. The young Frida seemed ready to jump at the chance to follow his lead. Her halted career in medicine, and the closed chapter of the *Prepa*, were replaced by the very public world of artists and their fans.

Gómez Arias returned from Europe, and Frida saw him from time to time, as well as her other *Prepa* comrades, but never as steadily as before. She kept up her painting, but without any particular schedule in mind and at her own pace. She supported the *Cachuchas* in their fight for autonomy for the university, but she now had other interests that took her elsewhere. Coaxed by Tina Modotti, Edward Weston, and her other new friends, Frida joined the Communist Party. She left behind the white blouse and simple dark skirt of her school days and sported red shirts with the hammer and sickle on them. She cut her hair short instead of wearing it in a bobbed style like her sisters always had. Since Cristina's stylish waves had been a point of envy, maybe Frida found a more provocative look by cutting off her feminine locks. Diego seemed impressed by her brashness, youth, and energy, and he remembered her pranks and jests of the days in the *Preparatoria*. She was unlike his other women, and he found her attentiveness gratifying. They began to spend more and more time together and on August 21, 1929, Frida Kahlo and Diego Rivera married in Coyoacán. She was 22 and he was 43. It was her first marriage and his first civil marriage. Everyone around them was taken by surprise.

The legend of this marriage partly had to do with what Frida's father Guillermo told her on her wedding day, and partly with what he is supposed to have told Diego. Frida recounted that her father called Rivera grotesque, "a fat, fat, fat Brueghel. [Your wedding is] like marrying an elephant with a dove" (Zamora 1987, 36). The image is an accurate one—Rivera's weight (both his physical size and his enviable social clout) and the lightness of Frida (her broken bones, failing health, and lack of means) are the first indications of what separated them. Aside from the obvious difference in size, though, the two newlyweds seemed to come from two different universes. His rowdiness and disorderly behavior pointed to an uncontrollable boy in a man's body, and her mischievousness showed that she was still playing the part of a protected, and just recently convalescent, daughter. He had traveled all over Europe while she had stayed in the vicinity of Mexico City all her life. He was closer to her father's age than her own. In a conversation just before the simple ceremony, Guillermo was said to have warned Rivera that Frida was "a little devil" (Alcántara and Egnolff 2005, 29) and that he should be very sure what he was getting into. Aware of how to manipulate others, Frida shared with Diego a love of willful misconduct.

Despite her father's warnings, neither backed out. Matilde and Guillermo were hardly happy about their daughter's marriage to an eccentric man many years her senior, and one who had lived with a number of women and had several children. If Matilde had been upset by her older daughter's running away from home with the help of Frida, she was totally distraught when Frida married Diego. Lupe Marín, one of the few other people present at the small ceremony, insinuated that Frida was no real rival to her and that Diego would miss her charms and her body. Maybe it was jealousy talking, or maybe age and experience. Frida's skinny leg was hidden under a long skirt and a *rebozo* (a woven Mexican shawl) borrowed from her maid for the occasion, so the comparison between these two women could not be made easily.

One of the few photos, if not the only one commemorating the event shows a fairly typical pose but with a fairly untypical couple. In a studio in Coyoacán—that it is indoors is made obvious by the Moorish arches and Gothic looking stained glass windows, with an Oriental rug underfoot—Diego stands to one side of Frida, with hat in hand and his arm around his new wife. Frida is seated on some sort of small chair or stool that is not visible, but which lets her assume the pose of a woman belonging to this man. If she was indeed the "devil" of the family as her father indicated, she was now someone else's responsibility. He is almost twice her height as he stands imposingly, filling more than half the space of the photo. Usually he was unkempt, messy to the extreme, especially when he was at work on a mural, but here he has lost his mane of hair and his head looks smaller compared to the height and width of the rest of his body. It was an occasion that required a haircut. He does not smile. He is dressed in a dark jacket and gray pants, a suit perhaps, with a somewhat wrinkled dress shirt and tie. Even this may even sound elegant until one looks at the details—the sleeves of the jacket are too long and cover his hand (a hand that holds a large, dark-colored hat); the tie is tied too short and doesn't reach the middle of his large, protruding stomach; his pants are hitched up high and held in place by a broad leather worker's belt with an enormous buckle. These individual items just don't go together. Maybe the suit is not his, but on loan from someone, the way Frida's shawl came from her maid, or was a recent purchase for the ceremony. It doesn't seem to fit him very well, and the pants have to be pulled up so that the shoes can peek out from beneath. He has dress shoes on, not the usual work boots, to mark the occasion.

Frida is modest and demure, seated with her hands folded on her lap as she did in childhood for her father's photos, but now without the hint of energy that would have thrust her out of the chair seventeen years earlier. She has lost her round cheeks, and her arms and legs—crossed and visible from under the flounces of the patterned dress—are very, very thin. The woven shawl is looped around her shoulders, and Frida wears a bracelet on one wrist, a beaded necklace, and dangling earrings. There is a small ribbon in her hair and she cocks her head to one side slightly, away from the side where Diego is standing, although this may not be a conscious choice of pose. There is no smile on Frida's face either and, except for the gala clothing and the recognizable type of studio scene, one would not think that a happy event was being recorded by this photograph. It is, however, a standard portrait of a traditional event in Mexico; the participants, however, are less than traditional.

After the wedding ceremony, the real celebration began and Diego drank until the wee hours of the morning. Guests recounted that Frida fled to her parents' house, telling them that her new husband had shot his pistol into the air, become loud and raucous, offended the guests, and broke several belongings of Roberto Montenegro, who had hosted the reception. Diego and Frida fought over his actions, she left, and they spent their wedding night apart. After a few days, they decided they could live together and Frida moved with Diego into his house on the elegant street *Reforma*, #104. They were right in the middle of the city and smack in the middle of the art world on the most elegant avenue in the heart of it all. There wasn't much furniture or decoration. They had a bed, a couple of tables given to them as gifts by her parents and friends, and a few archaeological pieces they put on display. Diego's former wife, Lupe Marín, visited their home often, helped Frida buy dishes and pots and pans in a nearby open air market, and kept vigil over her when she was ill. Rather than continuing to be jealous, Lupe took Frida under her wing and tried to explain to her what kind of person Rivera was. Rather than being rivals,

Marín and Kahlo commiserated like sisters over the difficult personality of this singular man. Lupe and Diego's two daughters formed a bond between the parents that never was to be broken, and Frida was just added into the mix. In fact, Lupe treated Frida like another child, since she was so much younger and had never left home before. Myths about Diego's insatiable sexual appetites were used to explain his need for so many women, and the inability of any one (or two) to satisfy him. Lupe even took Frida to a doctor that had treated Rivera for some undisclosed illness; he explained to her that Diego was a different kind of man who needed more of everything in life. She appeared to believe this, or at least used it as an excuse for his unfaithfulness.

As tradition would also have it, Frida tried to have children right away but this did not work out, much to her dismay. She told anyone who would listen that she wanted a little Diego, whether to keep Rivera with her or as proof of her importance to him for all his friends to see. Diego never spoke about Frida's burning desire, and some speculated he never wanted children at all. She told her friends that as a substitute for the child she did not have, she cooked, cleaned, and put colorful flowers on the table every day for Diego when he returned from his work. She carried lunch to him in straw and wicker baskets, and learned to cook foods he especially enjoyed. Frida also began to call Diego her child, and paintings she did in later years show her rocking him in her arms or nursing him like a baby. As time went by, Frida became less and less convinced of her role as a mother and increasingly focused on Diego and his art, then on her own artwork. Between medical problems and the personal issues between them, the subject of having a family eventually went silent. Maybe as their lives evolved, she thought a child would take her away from him rather than bringing them together, or maybe she thought he would be less pleased than she had first believed. Eventually, as a result of a combination of the accident, the scoliosis, and other more vague physical weaknesses, Frida would never confront him with the topic again. Some speculate she even had abortions to terminate pregnancies.

Gómez Arias and his friends found Frida's decision to marry Diego "monstrous" (Zamora 1987, 36). They had all known her as a lively and impetuous young woman, but the wedding seemed a great absurdity. The monstrosity they saw was similar to what her father had described on their wedding day. But Gómez Arias may also have been alluding to their breakup and to his knowledge of Frida as a woman who could seek revenge. Knowing that she was the last unmarried sister at home in the Blue House possibly gave him the idea of another motivation as well: to get out of that confining situation. Her extensive medical treatments since the accident in 1925 had kept her under the close supervision of her parents. Then her sisters had married and left with their spouses. Only *la niña Frida* was left in an empty house with parents who didn't get along that well. Since she wasn't attending school any longer, and the relationship with Gómez Arias was long over, Frida may have had escape on her mind when she married Diego. Or she may have killed two birds with one stone: Rivera could elevate her to the world stage of art and pay off her parents' accumulated debts on the Blue House. Then she could leave home with a clean conscience, knowing that her parents had been taken care of financially, and proceed to build her career in art. Diego had both money and fame, and he often treated Frida tenderly, like a little girl, calling her "*la niña de mis ojos*" (the apple of my eye, but also a play on words meaning the pupil of my eye). That he was equally tender and amorous with other women was something she put up with, at least in the beginning. After all, Lupe and the doctor had told her that Diego was not an ordinary man. Frida often said, even if she never believed it herself, that it would be impossible for her to marry a man that wasn't attractive to other women. She got her wish. Admirers would go to the foot of his scaffolding and flirt with him from below, even if he didn't descend to mingle among them. It was enough to stop work, chat about his talent, and return, gratified by the attention, to the daily project. His affairs were fleeting if numerous, and Diego said insistently that he had found in Frida his true other half. Even if there were other women in his life, Rivera always admitted that Frida was special. It may have taken a lifetime to convince him, but at her funeral Rivera looked genuinely alone and distraught without her.

As husband and wife, Frida and Diego set up their home in Mexico City, but they also began to travel. First on their itinerary, they visited as many cities and towns as they could in Mexico; later, they traveled abroad so that he could paint murals in San Francisco, Detroit, and New York. Commissions came flooding in. Shortly after the wedding, Diego received an invitation from the American Ambassador in Cuernavaca to paint a mural on the walls of the *Palacio de Cortés* (Cortés's palace) in that Mexican city. Since it was close to the capital where they lived, Frida and Diego made an excursion to check out the structure and the walls that would be his canvas.

A building of special historical importance, this palace was begun soon after the fall of the great Aztec city Tenochtitlán to the invading Spanish. It was destined to be a place where Cortés could collect all of the wealth brought to him annually by the subjects that were formerly under Aztec rule. It was finished in 1535, and sat atop a pyramid that predated it, an imposing structure high above ground-level buildings. This palace is the oldest example of civil architecture in Mexico, and exemplifies the problematic historical past of the nation. As a tribute to a conquering hero (at least in the eyes of the Spaniards), the palace was a constant reminder of Mexico's loss. Later a prison, then a center for the state government, the palace is now the *Museo Cuauhnáhuac* (Cuauhnáhuac Museum), housing Rivera's murals depicting the evils of the Spanish conquest of Mexico. This early project was a foundation for Rivera's later themes of oppression, colonization, political and social strife, and the almost mythical strength of those who survive even under the cruelest of invading forces. Increasingly popular with both state and national government figures, perhaps owing to the topics he decided to commemorate, Rivera was allowed to include what he wished in these murals. Most frequently, he depicted fearless and intrepid national heroes, crucial battles, or the depravity and corruption of the European conquerors and the bloodshed that occurred in what Europe often portrayed as civilizing missions. That he was able to put these images on public display in the palace originally built for Cortés is just one of many ironies in his career (but one that obviously worked out in his favor).

As Diego left each day to work on this monumental project, Frida visited historic sites in Cuernavaca and the surrounding towns. She became an expert in colonial architecture and got to know the local *cantina* (tavern) owners among whom she spent time and shared meals. As partners, especially on Sundays, Diego and Frida traveled to other places of importance in Mexican history, collecting sites and images for future work (in the case of Diego) or enjoying the celebrations and daily life of regular people in the country they admired and delighted in. They spent time together, yes, but not that much, since Rivera was busy almost every minute of the day and had to work on a schedule. Although it was less an imposed schedule than one of his own making, Diego was only Diego when he painted. So Frida obliged the artist and his creative talents, took him lunch on the scaffold, and offered positive comments on the progress of his murals. She did not paint. In the end, Diego's commission from the American Ambassador caused the expulsion of Rivera from the Communist Party in 1929. He was irate but kept the commission. Soon after, Frida resigned from the party, too, in support of her husband.

When Frida began painting again, it was because Diego spent so much time away from her on his mural assignments. In 1929, she painted a second self-portrait and *The Bus*, a small study of the passengers inside this typical mode of transportation. Not the infamous bus of her accident, this portrait of six riders on a wooden bus was painted from a vantage point across the aisle, observing them from close up and portraying the traditional dress and attitude of men and women on their way to work or on errands. The viewer of the scene sits as though one of the passengers among them. A mother and child, a man in a three-piece suit carrying a small bag, a worker in overalls, a middle class woman with a fiber shopping basket, and an attractive young woman in modern dress with high heels and a flowing red scarf complete the group. The colors are muted and there is the hint of a movement from the countryside to the city as we see the trees on one side of the bus turn into factories and smokestacks on the other. Perhaps as a frequent mode of travel for Frida and Diego, perhaps as a testimonial to the routine of daily life among a work force that was increasingly shuttled from the agricultural areas to the growing cities, this mode of transportation appears in a number of Frida's paintings.

Following this, *Self-Portrait in a Chair* (1930) shows Frida with short hair, her trademark earrings, and a look of deep sadness. Of course, she had depicted herself as a solitary woman in earlier self-portraits for Gómez Arias, but now she looks almost despondent. Her eyes were brown and had always been painted some shade of this color, but here the iris stands out in contrast with the stark white of the eye. Maybe the darkness is meant to reflect some notion of her impenetrability, some hint that even being close to Diego would not let him into her deepest thoughts. Maybe the straightforward little girl of her childhood photos has turned so far inward that access to her real emotions is no longer possible. Whatever the case, the glance of this painted figure closes off dialogue with her. There is a dot of light in each iris, a glimmer of someone or something she is looking at as she sits and watches herself in the mirror. But we only see her. The closely cut hair looks as if she has undergone some sort of therapy or suffered an illness, and it is harsher than in earlier portraits. (Her transformation upon joining the Communist Party alongside Rivera had changed her notion of how she should look and how she could represent Mexico in the eyes of the public.) Her dress is neutral and plain, with a scooped neckline, and the skin of her face, neck, and arms matches the earth tones of the background wall. The chair is the same color as her body and the walls, just a few shades darker. Here, Frida is one with the furniture and the décor of a house where she finds herself imprisoned once again. First the Blue House and now Rivera's home turned into a prison when she learned that exchanging one for the other did not make her happy. She had gotten what she wanted—the marriage to Diego—but she did not have the child for which she yearned. That child became the symbol of all that went wrong, even as time passed and the subject was suppressed in everyday conversation. Even Frida began to waver in her desire for a child as time went by.

A second set of artworks was done between 1930 and 1931; this time the subject matter returned to the couple, Frida and Diego. A 1930 ink drawing echoes their wedding photo, but now with Frida standing by Diego's side and holding his hand. Frida may have had the commemorative portrait to look at as she composed this scene, since she captured the original rigidity of Diego's stance, his large size, and uncomfortable clothing, and her slight turn of the head away from him. But they are standing now, so the full length of her dress is visible even if her feet disappear into the edge of the paper. Rivera wears work boots and not dress shoes, and his pants are cuffed to reveal shoelaces. His solid frame and her fragility are evident in their pose, and each stares at something other than their partner. Called simply *Diego and Frida,* this sketch may have been a preliminary plan for the 1931 oil painting on cloth entitled *Frieda and Diego Rivera,* their full married name as spouses, using the original spelling of her own first name and with her name appearing first this time. The portrait was painted in San Francisco, during the time when Rivera was commissioned to paint an allegory of the founding history of California at the Stock Exchange Lunch Club and then, a few months later, a mural depicting the building of the city of San Francisco at the California School of Fine Arts. When political difficulties intensified in Mexico in the late 1920s, and his allegiance to the Communist Party became a negative factor, Rivera decided to continue his work in the United States and accepted these projects in the Bay Area. During his first two commissions in San Francisco in 1930–1931, Rivera and Kahlo were extremely well received by both the political and artistic communities. In fact, their reception was so encouraging that Rivera returned to San Francisco in 1940, based on the success of his first period there, to execute the Pan American Unity mural for the Golden Gate International Exposition. This public work reflected his love for the city of San Francisco and his affection for the artists who had supported him when he had lost favor in Mexico.

Maybe alone again, even among the friendly and progressive groups that had invited them to California, or maybe thinking of the child she did not yet have, Frida turned to her own life for subject matter as she also turned to art to fill in the empty hours. Increasingly, she missed Mexico. In this painting, the third after the photograph and the drawing of the couple, Frida made Diego look more imposing and even less cordial. Frida, in a red shawl and dark flounced dress, seems even smaller. The general characteristics of the relationship are still there, but something is slightly different about them. The couple is subdued, not celebratory; the woman is holding his hand but she places hers gingerly on top of his massive hand. He carries a palette and paint brushes, she clutches the *rebozo* and tilts her head ever so slightly toward him (not away as before). In the couple, he has a profession and an imposing presence, since he clutches the artists' materials, but she is just an accessory. Her diminutive feet—too small to actually carry her anywhere it seems—create the impression that she is floating in air, not standing squarely on the ground. Neither is seated; instead, both stand on a dark floor with a fairly intense blue wall behind them. The only thing breaking these large patches of color that surround them is a small dove that floats above Frida's head, carrying the faint traces of a white banner in its beak. Their faces betray no emotion, but their identities are clear: he is a painter; she is Mexican. Her clothing was all that was left of her former life as she navigated the waters of San Francisco society. The caption for the scene says that this was painted for Mr. Albert Bender, a patron of the arts and trustee of Mills College. Although an insurance broker by trade, his reputation as a supporter of artists from many places earned him international respect. Frida writes in the caption that Bender is "our friend," and that the content of the portrait is "Yo, Frieda Kahlo, con mi adorado esposo Diego Rivera" (I, Frieda Kahlo with my adored husband Diego Rivera). She is exact in pointing out that they are both there, but the adoration is not very visible on their faces.

Diego's compulsion to work all hours of the day and night was fed by commissions for murals in other U.S. states, and these took the couple to Detroit and New York after their sojourn in San Francisco. At the Detroit Institute of Arts, Rivera worked on a fresco cycle entitled *Detroit Industry*, honoring the contributions of Henry Ford to the technological progress of the modern United States. The industrial heritage of the Motor City is visible in two large wall panels dedicated to the races that came together to produce the work force of American culture, the automotive industry as an impulse for change and advancement, the other industries of Detroit that were forged into a twentieth-century powerhouse, and the River Rouge plant where the 1932 Ford V8 was manufactured. As he had in Mexico, Rivera represented these layers of industrial progress in subsequent layers of images, culminating at the top of the wall in the strong arms and hands of the laborers whose work in the underground portions of the panels comes together in the final harmony of product and producer. Rivera considered these frescoes, commissioned by Edsel Ford, to be some of his most successful work. He was celebrated with continuous festivities and honors.

In the meantime, Frida remained at his side, but was about to be faced with another set of health issues that would compound her isolation and sense of loss. Although she had won Diego over from all his other female admirers, she had not produced the child she so desired (whether he had the same desire by this time is unclear, however). And at the same time, she was desperately afraid of having a child given her own medical condition. In 1932, Frida suffered a lesion on one toe, and there was always the chance it would spread or become infected. While she thought about children, she also feared the consequences. It turned out that she would not have much choice. In mid-1932, Frida was interned at the Henry Ford Hospital suffering from a severe hemorrhage. Gynecologists diagnosed a spontaneous abortion, or miscarriage, one of several she would suffer in her lifetime. (Some have conjectured that Frida herself may have induced some of them, but there is no evidence in her diaries or anywhere else for such a conclusion.)

In *Henry Ford Hospital, My Birth*, and *Frida and the Abortion*, Frida used the anatomical studies of her days at the *Prepa* to put the physical pain and mental anguish triggered by this crisis into very graphic form. Either prone in a hospital bed, surrounded by malformed fetuses, remnants of technology, pools of blood, and shattered pelvic bones, with the city of Detroit (where Diego was working) far off in the distance; witnessing her own bloody birth under a portrait of the *Mater Dolorosa* (Mary, the suffering mother); or carved up into organs and pools of entrails tied together with bodily fluids such as tears and blood, Frida made her anguish visible for all to see. Her heart may look like an artist's palette (in *Frida and the Abortion*), and she almost literally did put her heart into her work, but the creation of the images did not seem to be an adequate substitute for the impossibility of creating a son or daughter. Signed Frieda Rivera and not Frieda Kahlo, this lithographic testimony to her physical pain was accurate in its details down to the texture of the skin, and so authenticated both her suffering and her talent. At the same time as it documented historical moments of her life, Frida's art began to take on its most original characteristic: a way to document the hidden dimensions of pain, a vehicle for a woman's most dramatic internal dilemmas. Turning herself inside out, Frida made spectators look at the inner workings of the human body as art. Just as Diego glorified the workers and the original inhabitants of the Americas before the contamination of the Spanish Conquest, Frida found her subject matter close at hand. Her body and the medical technologies that would invade it would do battle for the next two decades. It wasn't the first time that art became her therapy.

Chapter 3

A WORLD OF DREAMS AND NIGHTMARES

In early September 1932, as Frida faced her ongoing gynecological complications, she also had to deal with her mother's death. She was far from home, and felt more abandoned than ever when she received the news of Matilde's serious illness. She and her mother had never been close, but her detachment from the family compounded the gravity of her mother's situation for her. Frida had always yearned for more constant contact with her family, her friends, and her beloved Mexico, but in Detroit she was alone much of the time. Diego always had his art, but Frida had only Diego. And he was not someone to be counted on, at least not as she expected him to be. His retrospective at the Museum of Modern Art had added to his status and prestige, but Frida remained in the shadows as Mrs. Rivera, the small and almost invisible wife of the great Mexican painter. Like her wedding portrait of the couple, he stood on solid ground but she floated above it.

The matter became even more complicated when Diego was awarded an enviably large and important commission to work on a mural for the brand new complex of buildings called Rockefeller Center in the heart of Manhattan, for it meant he had to postpone a return home. Rivera was thrilled to be the center of attention and he saw no reason to interrupt his chain of successes. Begun in 1928, the architectural project named after John D. Rockefeller was a monumental undertaking using only private money. It was originally envisioned as a new home for the Metropolitan Opera, but when plans were changed, the rest of the buildings were put up without including this one. The fourteen Art Deco styled buildings were meant to pay tribute to the family and its power as much as to the modern constructions filling the city as it slowly emerged from the stock market crash of 1929. In the fiscal crisis, bankers withdrew support from the project, but private Rockefeller oil company stock was tapped to cover the expenses. The invitation was beyond what Rivera had expected after San Francisco and Detroit, when the couple planned to go back to Mexico City, and the temptation was irresistible. He accepted the offer to cover the walls of one interior with frescoes, so Frida and Diego set out from Detroit for New York City. Even with the news of Matilde Kahlo's illness (some say it was cancer, others say it was a complication of gall bladder surgery), Diego did not want to leave New York, so Frida left for Coyoacán accompanied by her friend Lucienne Bloch, the daughter of a Swiss composer, who she had befriended in San Francisco. They arrived at the Blue House on September 8; a week later Frida's mother was dead. She stayed in Mexico with Bloch until October 21, then they returned to Diego in New York. He had been busy in her absence and, as long as her companion was a woman and not a man, he did not pay much attention to the whole issue.

Although Frida had returned to painting while in San Francisco and Detroit, and had made important connections with collectors such as Albert Bender and the physician Dr. Leo Eloesser who would remain her friend throughout the rest of her life, she did not like many of the men and women she met in the United States. This was particularly true of the upper classes who invited them to gala dinners in Rivera's honor and who, to Frida, seemed to waste their money while the poor lived in terrible conditions. In the decade of the Depression, this would have been a detail that stood out to someone like Frida, who came from a country with similar economic woes. A few, such as Lucienne Bloch, took to her right away, but Frida was more shy and retiring than many women her age and did not mix with the arts crowds as Diego did. After all, she was only 25 years old and had spent much of her adult life either in bed convalescing or married to Diego. His Detroit murals were the subject of much attention, but Frida's work was ignored by all, including Rivera. Only Dr. Eloesser, her physician and sometimes more of a confessor, paid any attention to her and Frida may have used her ailments to perpetuate their contact. That she became fairly obsessed with medical procedures, popular cures, and the minute details of her body was made evident in her art and in her correspondence with this pioneer in the field of thoracic surgery, who dedicated a lot of his energy to the poor and the indigent. Dr. Eloesser was paid with a painting Kahlo did of him, and this system of medical care in exchange for artistic creation remained their primary means of contact.

As she got to know New York City, the recently inaugurated Museum of Modern Art was a fascinating place for Frida, but it was little consolation for her homesickness. Frida spent some of her time among the avant-garde artists' groups, and she made personal connections that would later be very useful to her, but she felt like a constant outsider. Feeding both her longing for Mexican culture and her growing desire to be provocative in a land that did not touch her heart, Frida did not retire into the woodwork or try and blend in socially; instead, she chose to stand out. As she had done during her short time at the *Prepa* as a teenager, Frida counteracted her boredom by agitating others with her words or her appearance. As she had donned the sports cap that the *Cachuchas* had used to identify their group, so she cultivated visible signs of being "Mexican" while in New York. If society people were going to try and ignore her, Frida was not going to let them get away with it.

During the couple's stay in the United States in the 1930s, Frida continued to dress in her *Tehuana* costumes, her jade pendants and earrings, and strolled up and down Fifth Avenue to attract attention. If Diego had previously requested that she use this style of dress as a marker for the artistic community in Mexico City, Frida now used it to promote herself as an object of curiosity for New York high society. She hated to be invisible, and relished the surprise and comments of style makers and fashion designers when they noticed her. The diminutive Mrs. Rivera standing behind the painter turned into the Mrs. Rivera of the rose-colored floor-length embroidered skirts, peasant blouses, hair ribbons, and shoulder-brushing dangling earrings. She became synonymous with the exotic and the different, and she loved it. In 1938, when writers from the French edition of *Vogue* magazine asked to put a photograph of her hand with its many rings on all her fingers on the cover of an issue, she readily accepted. That sealed her image as a unique woman who might even set a trend. What was still missing, however, was recognition of Frida as a unique artist.

As Frida dealt with designers and what she called rich "snobs," Diego had to face criticism of his work for Rockefeller Center. Entitled *Man at the Crossroads*, his murals included separate panels of Lenin and the workers on one side of a large scene with the wealthy giants of American industry on the other. Needless to say, the Rockefeller family, as a scion of American business and investment, was not pleased. Rivera would not change the content or the commentary, and the Rockefellers stood firm against such political statements on the walls of their New York complex. After a tempestuous series of encounters, Rivera received compensation for what he had finished, was removed from the project shortly thereafter, and was publicly reprimanded for his refusal to comply with their wishes. When the artist placed wealthy patrons of the arts with rich industrialists, he obviously categorized those who had commissioned his own work in this criticized group. That was too much. In 1934, the murals were painted over. The Mexican government made some sort of restitution for this failed project by offering Rivera the walls of the top floor of the Art Deco *Bellas Artes* building in Mexico City so that he could paint a reproduction of the erased New York frescoes. This he did and they remain on display for all to see. Now christened *Man Controls the Universe or Man in the Time Machine,* they reflect Rivera's previous themes without any change of social or political critique.

After her mother's death, Frida yearned to go home. The oil painting and collage entitled *My Dress Hangs There* offers all the clues we need to feel the depth of her loneliness. This was the only work she produced in 1933 when Rivera was dedicated wholeheartedly to his mural projects. In this tiny painting—it is only 18 × 19 inches—the wealth of details is impressive. In the center of the frame, hanging in front of a dense group of high rise buildings, and right below the New York Stock Exchange whose front steps have become a graph of the ups and downs of the American economy, hangs a *Tehuana* dress just like the one Frida was recognized for wearing day in and day out. Now on a hanger and not covering her body, the dress is a stand-in for the person who has departed, left it behind, abandoned it to its new environment, or just plain decided it was enough to represent her and she was no longer needed. On either side of the dress are architectural columns, trophies, toilets, gas pumps, garbage cans filled to the brim, smoke stacks, water towers, steam pipes, the Brooklyn Bridge, bread lines (in photos cut out from newspapers and pasted on the surface of the board), a church steeple, and a blazing fire covering a building in flames and smoke. This inferno is a reference to the March 25, 1911, fire at the Triangle Shirtwaist Company, which claimed the lives of 146 young immigrant workers who had been confined in deplorable conditions and failed to escape when the fire broke out. The doors had been locked so they would not be able to take breaks during work, and the disaster was just a question of time. One of the greatest tragedies since the beginning of the Industrial Revolution, Frida could not overlook it as an example of the great American dream turned into a nightmare. Alongside the beautiful constructions of New York, she indicated in this small work all of the death and suffering under the surface of the glittering city of Manhattan, which stands in the background as the destination of the steamship crossing into New York harbor, with the symbolic Statue of Liberty in the distance. The many dreamers who embark on the journey turn into the endless lines of hungry workers desperately seeking jobs. Dangling in the middle of this golden dream turned into dark reality is Frida's empty dress. By the end of 1933, she has seen enough of the city and its people to feel herself emptied and suspended in mid-air, just waiting for Diego to finish so they could return home. On December 20, 1933 they finally sailed for Mexico—via Cuba—and Frida's wish came true.

The Riveras moved into new homes in San Angel, a quaint suburb southeast of Mexico City. First founded by the Carmelites in the seventeenth century as a rural refuge for meditation, San Angel was fast becoming a place for the wealthiest inhabitants of Mexico City to build country estates. With his new fame and fortune from their years in the United States, Rivera wanted a studio worthy of his status. He had a studio plus house built by the famous architect Juan O'Gorman in the Functionalist style and began to hold court there. People of the art world, politicians, and movie stars all congregated there, with Diego the center of attention. Today, this structure of real utility and convenience for a working artist has opened as an art gallery and a cultural center. Following the tradition of paying homage to the talent and fame of figures of importance in Mexican history, Rivera's studio has been made available to generations of artists. The studio was a place for Diego and not Frida, and obviously more a space for art than a home. Frida had O'Gorman create a smaller studio for her right next door. Rivera was less than pleased to give up his newfound celebrity, and in San Angel he lapsed into long unproductive periods when he did not leave the larger building. While Frida got what she had wanted for so long, Diego was now making her pay the price for returning. If they had seen little of each other in their several years abroad, this continued back in Mexico with the added dimension of Rivera's feeling of resentment over having to relinquish his international status. Only at the end of 1934, almost a full year later, did Diego return to his frescoes for the stairwell of the National Palace; Frida continued to drift. And each now inhabited a separate—if connected—space.

But all was not calm with Frida after their arrival either, because she began to suspect that Rivera was having another affair. As a newlywed, she had heard of his adventures and exploits with women, but maybe in her innocence she thought that she would be the one to change his ways. Not only was she underestimating his need for attention, she also overestimated her power over him. Frida was to receive the shock of her life when she discovered that not only was Diego involved with another woman, it was her sister Cristina. She was devastated and felt betrayed by both of them. Like the hopeful new arrivals into New York harbor, Frida's dreams of a joyous return home were dashed.

If all of this grief weren't enough, Frida's health once again worsened. She had another miscarriage and, shortly after, her foot became infected again. In an effort to end the pain in her toes and the constantly recurring infections, she had all five toes on her right foot amputated. This seemed a remedy for the circulatory problems in her legs and feet once and for all, although it would not be the end of her problems. These physical complications were more easily addressed, though, than the betrayal by her husband and her sister. Rivera refused to end the affair with Cristina and all of their friends were aware of this turn of events. When Frida went to the National Palace to see the three-part mural he had been painting dedicated to the historical *Epic of the Mexican People,* she found that Diego had put their difficult situation on display for all to see. Among the many, many faces of the workers lining the mural on the side of the stairway, both Cristina and Frida appear. He had used them as the faces of women educating the masses and joining in heroic acts during the Revolution and after. Rivera showcased his lover Cristina, placing her in front of Frida, and partially obscuring her with her two children (the children Frida did not have) to whom she is reading. This was another blow to Frida's ego. As she wrote of her suffering to her old friend Dr. Eloesser in San Francisco, Frida admitted that she had lost Diego to Cristina and that she had never understood what he wanted from her. Her words show that she blamed herself—she said she forgave Cristina—more than anyone for this situation. Throughout 1934, Frida did not paint a thing. She was paralyzed by sadness and by being cast aside by Rivera so easily.

1935 would start out differently for Frida. Many Mexican newspapers carried vivid stories of the bloody murder of a wife by her husband. It seems that he had been angered by her and took revenge by cutting her all over with a knife. Frida made that violent subject matter her own, using the marital squabble as a means of commenting on her own situation with Diego. She painted *Unos cuantos piquetitos* (Just a few little nicks), maybe as a metaphor for her own physical pain and emotional grief, and definitely an outlet for her resentment toward the relationship between Diego and Cristina. In the painting, once again a small canvas only 15 × 19 inches, a nude woman lies stretched out on a simple, low bed, with one shoe on and one missing. Her body is immobile in the middle of pools of blood that splash out on the sheets and across the floor. A man, knife in hand, stands over her with a grin on his face. Even his teeth are visible as he admires his handiwork. Covered in her blood, he stands above her as a dove flies over them both, trailing a ribbon that gives us the title: "Just a few little nicks." His underplaying of the scenario by smiling, and the title's evident ironic tone, frame the poor dead woman. A victim of his weapon of choice—here a knife, perhaps; Kahlo was cut by Rivera's actions—she has been silenced by the large quantity of diminutive nicks that turned into such a fatal mess. The painting is disturbing in its overkill: the colors, the details, and the snide grin unite to tell the story of a woman who had succumbed to the will of her husband. And he did her in little by little, not all at once. By that time, Frida had spent almost six years married to Diego and the wounds, like those of the dead woman whose body she painted, had accumulated until they had reached the end of the line. Frida must have identified with the victim she painted.

Such scenes with morbid details of violence and death found their way into her paintings for the next several years. A dead child became the subject of a 1937 canvas entitled *El difuntito Dimas Rosas a los tres años de edad* (Poor little Dimas Rosas, Dead at the Age of Three). The cult to dead children was alive and well in Mexico at the time, as reflected in both photography and in the more traditional painted scenes. It was customary to create a vivid portrait of the dead child before one forgot what he or she looked like and to evoke the grief caused by an early demise. As a remembrance of the angelic child taken away too soon, Dimas Rosas, with his half-closed eyes and innocent face, fit in perfectly with Frida's personal life as well. Death and children (or the lack of them) had been in the center of her thoughts since the accident of 1925. Now a full decade later, Frida still carried with her the scars of her brush with death; Diego became the second tragedy to befall her and his betrayal made her turn to the image of death once again.

In late 1938, the death of socialite Dorothy Hale filled Frida's mind with the fragility of life one more time. A woman Frida had met in New York, and a close friend of Isamu Noguchi, who would be Frida's lover when she returned to the United States after leaving Diego, Hale had lived a charmed life and her suicide was a historical fact. She had suffered through some unfortunate personal relationships, and had seen no way out but taking her own life. In Frida's version of the event, turbulent clouds fill the painting with a generic skyscraper in the background. A pale woman dressed in an even paler garment flies through the air head first, entwined in the clouds and the mist. At the bottom of the painting lies the broken body of Dorothy Hale after reaching the ground. Now flesh-colored and less white, with a dress as dark as the ground on which she fell, Hale lies dead with her face toward the viewer. Someone—rumor has it that in real life it was Noguchi himself—placed a small bunch of white flowers on her in memory of the woman that had been. This violent event fills the canvas and spills out onto the frame of Frida's painting *El suicidio de Dorothy Hale* (Dorothy Hale's Suicide), drawing the spectator into the scene. Another woman had been done in, a victim of the actions (or rejection) of a man to whom she had given her heart.

In addition to these tragic images, Frida returned to her self-portraits; this time they had a new look. In *Recuerdo* (I Remember, or Souvenir) of 1937, she places herself full length in the middle of a canvas, surrounded by dark blue storm clouds and, under her feet, an ocean with waves lapping on one side and a dark brown shoreline of a continent on the other. One foot has turned into a sailboat and is about to slip away into the sea; the other is planted on the earth close to a very large and very bloody heart that has been removed from some enormous body and left there. A sword with a tiny winged angel sitting on its handle pierces her chest where her heart would be. Frida is shown in a stark white dress—apparently one lent to her in fact by Lucienne Bloch—and a modern short printed jacket. She has no arms, but an abandoned *Tehuana* dress to her left encases one of her arms in its tunic; this arm reaches out to entwine itself in her sleeve. To Frida's right, in the distance, is a schoolgirl's outfit of a bright white shirt and navy blue skirt. This ensemble contains her other arm, which also reaches out but does not extend far enough to touch the central figure. Part of Frida's past is encapsulated by each form of dress: first, her school days; then, her time as Mrs. Rivera. Frida's face is covered with tears. Her hair is cut very short and the only recognizable trait from previous portraits is the single winged eyebrow. Had she left things behind—clothing, years of her life, personal relationships—even if they tore her limbs from her torso as she tried to go on? Or did this show that she dragged her past with her, hanging on to the severed arms in fear of losing everything? *I Remember* as the title of this transitional work would link the pain of remembering with the act of creation. And *Souvenir* (just a variation on the translation of the Spanish title) would underline the fact that nothing disappeared, but instead was turned into a part of what Frida would eventually become. In this very small painting, barely 12" by 15" in size, Frida condensed her life into art, her dreams into the nightmare of the bloody and ripped out heart. This displaced organ covered the earth with blood and, as a metaphor, its exaggerated size showed the weight of its emotional suffering. These works signaled the beginning of an extremely productive time for Frida. Between 1937 and 1949, she produced many of the self-portraits for which she is now known, and many of the images identified with her. These include vines, tropical flowers, her pet monkey, still life paintings with lush fruit, floating red hair ribbons, and colorful indigenous clothing. Her outward look defined her inner emotions.

In 1935, the affair between Diego and Cristina had become so intolerably obvious to her friends and family that Frida moved out of the studio-house in San Angel and into an apartment of her own in Mexico City.

Her long hair had been a particular attraction for Rivera, so when they separated, Frida had her hair cut very short. Until 1937, when she began to let it grow back, Frida made her self-portraits document this visible change as her life began to change. Sometimes her locks of hair appear on the floor and sometimes she just looks straight out, her face framed by waves of dark hair that reach only her ear lobes. She turned to women artists for support as she distanced herself from Diego and Cristina. Frida began drinking heavily, as a 1935 photograph of her taken by Lucienne Bloch shows: Frida cradles a large bottle of Cinzano in her arms and points to it for all to see. In part as revenge against Diego, she began having affairs of her own with other men and women she had known from both recent and earlier times. It was said that Diego did not mind her affairs with women, but that he was jealous of her relations with other men. In an attempt to put more space between them, a greater space than their side-by-side studios or her city apartment offered, Frida left Mexico City for New York. This time, there was no Diego. It was certainly ironic that the woman who had yearned to go home now went back to the city Diego had not wanted to leave. Frida optimistically held out hope for a resolution of their romantic conflicts, but found solace in the arms of sculptor Isamu Noguchi in New York. For eight months in 1935, Kahlo was loved and comforted by Noguchi. Frida reciprocated this love, but always said she felt even more for Diego. And it was Rivera that she eventually returned to. This fatal attraction would bring them back together, but the mid-1930s found Frida on her own in the United States in the company of a number of avant-garde artists. Their recognition of her talent would raise her self-esteem as a painter.

Another of her strongest ties in New York City was to the Hungarian-American photographer Nikolas Muray. Muray took several close-up shots of Frida and even convinced her to pose partially nude for him. His photograph of her nude torso is aesthetically pleasing, and erotically enticing. Like Noguchi, Muray was captivated by Frida both as an exotic woman and as a budding artist. He gave her the attention she had craved from Rivera. Their intimacies led to Frida's joining the men's circle of friends and to much speculation about Rivera's jealousy. While Diego did not sacrifice his art for her, he did not want her to find someone else to take his place. In his eyes, women could never do that for Frida, but men younger and more dashing than him might. One story had Rivera arriving in New York to find Kahlo with Noguchi, and threatening him with a pistol. Maybe with her artistically talented father Guillermo in mind, or maybe to get closer to someone in a culture that was not hers, Frida found good companions in Muray and Noguchi. Alienated from what she called *Gringolandia*, Frida found other immigrants like herself with whom to spend this difficult time in her life.

Already inside the Hollywood establishment, Muray had promoted the use of theatrical portraits by performers and celebrities such as Greta Garbo as miniature glossy calling cards. Following Edward Steichen's 1928 visit to Hollywood and his success with such photos, the magazine *Vanity Fair* sent Muray to California to continue this tradition. As a recognized independent photographer working in New York, Muray had acquired a strong reputation for headshots and figure portraits. He was at the center of one of the most radical artistic movements of the times. From 1919 to 1921 Berenice Abbott, the future photographer and compiler of the *Changing New York* archive that included representations of the modern city through 1935, supported herself as an artist's model, posing for photographers Nikolas Muray and Man Ray. While Kahlo did not support herself in that way, she was enticed to pose for Muray for other reasons. These might have included the scandal that a nude photograph of her torso would cause (to Rivera or to others) and the satisfaction of being considered a beauty worthy of that medium. More concerned with the health of her ailing body, Muray's attention to its erotic elements would go a long way to allay Frida's anguish over being unattractive. Frida had thought she could not compete with Cristina, the prettier and more alluring sister. Losing Diego to Cristina proved that. Now, Noguchi and Muray contradicted that and gave Frida new confidence.

As for Muray, Noguchi, André Breton, Marcel Duchamp, and other Dadaists and Surrealists, the New York art scene was full of creative possibilities for Frida. As Diego once again immortalized his vision of the working classes in frescoes, other painters and photographers were engaged in more radical experimentation with how to represent forms and figures. Frida may have ended up using a more naïve style in her own works, but she was well acquainted with cutting edge, less realistic and more experimental forms. The monumental style of the muralists was not for her; she never produced frescoes and rarely painted on a large scale. Frida did not produce many paintings up to the middle of the decade of the 1930s, but her short break with Rivera and her turn toward the international art scene would begin to change that. Between 1937 and 1938, Kahlo did a prolific amount of work that attracted the attention of Breton as well as Julien Levy, the owner of a prestigious New York gallery. In fact, Breton was especially taken by both the style and the themes (self-portraits) of Frida's art; in a short phrase made famous throughout the years, he announced to all that "The art of Frida Kahlo is a ribbon around a bomb." In 1938 and 1939, Kahlo had one-woman shows in Mexico City, New York (at the Levy Gallery), and in Paris. Rivera was struggling; between 1936 and 1940 he received no commissions.

Frida's return to Mexico and to Diego was in many ways triumphant. Her art was more publicly recognized than ever and she had made a name for herself abroad. After returning to Mexico City and to their conjoined studios, Frida did not cease traveling alone to the United States or to Europe to be present at her gallery openings. Even when her health declined further, she asked to be transported by ambulance and by stretcher so as not to miss an opening. On the other hand, Diego began to suffer from health issues of his own. Extreme diets did not keep weight off, and bad eating habits added to his drinking. Frida and Diego both drank heavily, but that did not necessarily bring them together. When the exiled revolutionary Leon Trotsky was invited by Mexican president Lázaro Cárdenas—at Rivera's insistence—to take refuge in Mexico, Diego could not go. In January, 1937, Frida was sent in his place to the gulf port of Tampico to greet Trotsky and his wife, Natalya Sedova, and to transport them back to Mexico City. Rather than in the Riveras' studios, Trotsky and Sedova would stay with Frida's father in the Blue House until Trotsky's assassination by secret agent Ramón Mercader on August 20, 1940. Sent by Stalin, Mercader would successfully accomplish what many others had tried to do.

Frida's mother's death a few years earlier had left Guillermo a widow, and he had been living alone. His houseguests were not the run of the mill type, but their presence did manage to get Frida over to see him more than she had done before. Frida was well aware of Diego's fascination with Trotsky, and with the strings Rivera had pulled to get the government to grant him asylum. After her time away in New York, she may have found that spending time with Trotsky was a perfect way to get back into his heart. Frida was an escort, a companion, and a self-assured young woman. At 29, she was half Trotsky's age and maybe their obvious differences were part of their mutual attraction. The result of their meeting was that Kahlo and Trotsky carried on an affair for several months. One of the greatest ironies of this was the fact that they could not meet where Rivera would find them, and they could not meet under the nose of Guillermo Kahlo in the Blue House, so they met in secret at Cristina's house. The same sister who had torn Diego from Frida gave them the space to hold their liaison. Was this Frida's revenge on Diego? Was it Cristina's revenge on Diego? Nothing was certain except the obligation Frida claimed she had to Diego and the obligation Trotsky felt toward Natalya. One thing was sure: there had been enough passion between them that they feared both marriages would be broken up; and so the two of them backed off. Now, Frida had been the object of affection of two handsome young men—Muray and Noguchi—and one charismatic revolutionary. Images of desire began to burn in the lush foliage of her paintings and in the renewed energy with which she dedicated herself to her work.

On Trotsky's birthday in 1937, Kahlo presented him with the gift of a painting. Rather than a painting with a political theme, it was *Self-Portrait Dedicated to Leon Trotsky* or *Between the Curtains*. A bit larger than her usual work, and on canvas rather than board or tin or wood, this is a full-length celebration of Frida in all her glory. Framed between the curtains of the title, pale green and elegantly tied back to reveal Frida as if she had just appeared on stage, the artist looks out proudly. She is dressed in the deep rose color of traditional Mexican façades and home interiors. It is a flattering tone for her face, neck, and hands, which emerge from the folds of an elegant peasant skirt and blouse combination, enveloped in a *huipil*, the long shawl native women wear to carry their babies. Much more exquisite and refined than the borrowed outfit in which she married Diego, these items of clothing contribute to Frida's mystery and natural beauty. Her neckline is enhanced by a pin worn in the style of colonial era portraits of elegant ladies of the court, and she sports the recognizable dangling gold earrings. Her hair is no longer short, but braided and pinned up with pink ribbons and flowers. These blossoms are echoed in the small bouquet she carries in her hands. As usual, Frida is not smiling. Portraiture was a serious art, and for this to be an elegant gift for formal presentation, it would have to be as posed as Guillermo's earlier photos of Frida had been. If there is any doubt as to who this is for, Frida carries a scrolled paper in her left hand: "For Leon Trotsky, with all my affection, I dedicate this painting, November 7, 1937. Frida Kahlo. In San Angel, Mexico." Frida gave her self-portrait to Trotsky as an actress might have handed her calling card to her fans. She looks young, assured, exotic, and as enticing as the Mexican landscape Trotsky would have found upon his arrival in Tampico. It must have been difficult to break off their relationship, but he was left with this very personal memento that he kept hanging in his study until the day he died.

After the affair with Trotsky ended, Frida began to paint fulltime. A recurring theme of the period between 1937 and 1938 was motherhood, as seen in several disturbing works. *Yo y mi muñeca* (My Doll and I) shows a return to a forlorn figure of a woman sitting on a barren piece of furniture. This time she is accompanied by a naked baby doll. They are posed primly in an empty room whose terracotta color surrounds them both like the earth surrounds Frida in earlier portraits. It is speculated that she might have had another miscarriage and that this toy was a stand-in for the child who continued to be absent from her life. Whether true or not, the serenity of Frida's face and its lack of emotion—no tears are visible—may mark a point for her when the frustration of childlessness was already a fact of life. A doll, or Diego, she had two substitutes for children. A second self-portrait from 1937, *Mi nana y yo* (My Nurse and I), reversed the relationship between the figures in the scene. This time around, Frida is the child being nursed by a dark-skinned woman wearing a mask. Attaching her adult head to a diminutive child's body, Frida takes all the power away from herself and places it in the forces of nature surrounding the two: earth, wind, water, roots, vegetation, milk, and the love of the arms that encircle her tiny body. Eventually sold to the actor Edward G. Robinson to add to his art collection, Frida adored how this painting turned out, especially in what she saw as her helplessness being supported by the strength of the nanny. She also needed the money. It finally sold in 1941, with several other paintings from the same period.

Along with a small, very soft, and romanticized portrait of Diego made in 1937, Frida did a tiny painting of Alberto Misrachi, a well-known bookseller and close friend of Diego and Frida. Both are composed as what would be head shots in photography, close-ups of the two men that reveal the affection felt by Frida toward both. Misrachi would later play an important role in her life when Frida's medical bills began mounting once again and she needed an agent to help sell her work. Misrachi also advanced her money for these expenses, and she was a very grateful friend. In addition to the portraits of these two men, Frida turned to still-life painting and chose for her compositions the most succulent fruits of the Mexican markets. Among the exotic fruits she painted were the *pitaya*, a pink and green fruit of one of Mexico's indigenous cacti, figs, pomegranates, plums, and even an ear of corn or two to make sure no one would be confused about the land they came from. Some critics call these paintings her most "Mexican" for their ties to the earth and for their vivid colors, sometimes placed on a table or on a ceramic dish, with recognizable Mexican cloudy skies behind it all. If she had smoothed over any imperfections in her paintings of Misrachi and Rivera, she also romanticized her homeland through these luscious examples of daily fare. Not all was the flora and fauna of a life renewed after returning home, but even though she painted memories of open wounds on her legs and feet, Frida moved from these tragedies to a focus on her face. Over the next decade, she painted the majority of the self-portraits for which she has been recognized.

In October 1938, Frida traveled back to New York City to put together the one-woman art show promised her earlier by Julien Levy. There were about twenty-five paintings in the collection and she sold at least a portion of them. That encouraged her to think about herself as an artist. After having received payment in dollars (a harder currency than pesos) from Edward G. Robinson, Frida looked forward to selling her work after having given it away for free for so long. She had used small paintings to pay off debts and as gifts to friends for birthdays and other special events. She considered this exhibit and sale public recognition of her quality as an artist, and in many ways they placed her among the ranks of those who received commissions, like Diego Rivera. What the Levy Gallery exhibit did was display Frida's paintings for the international critics who, for the most part, admired her talent. Rivera wrote to several of them to add his support and this, in turn, brought Frida to the attention of the Surrealist painter and writer André Breton, who invited her to Paris for a retrospective of her work in the spring of 1939. While her link with Surrealism was more fortuitous than planned or intellectual, the primitive look of much of this radical art movement would offer Frida a place for what she painted and a way for those who referred to her work to categorize it.

The backing of Muray and Noguchi, the recognition by Trotsky, the sales of her paintings to international art collectors, none of her international fame and connections were enough to convince her to accept Breton's offer right away. She wasn't sure what to do and sent Diego a letter to ask for his advice. Diego's response from Mexico City to Frida in New York told her to do whatever would make her happy, since that would also please him. Frida remained unconvinced and spent some months thinking it over. She did finally decide to go to Paris to add her work to the exhibit called *Mexique* at the Pierre Colle Gallery. As a tribute to Mexican culture, which had truly fascinated the Surrealist writers and painters as more liberated and closer to a natural world than European cultures, this collection of a variety of objects attempted to capture the spirit of the New World through the eyes of its inhabitants. As Breton saw it, this instinctive and free vision of Mexican art included paintings by Kahlo, pre-Columbian stone sculpture, and plenty of examples of popular arts and crafts including tall *papier maché* Judas dolls and smaller devotional images such as *ex votos*. The *ex votos* were tiny silver images of arms, legs, hands, eyes, or other features of the human body left by the devoted on altars in appreciation of miracles and cures that had been granted. A mixture of religious faith and local handicraft, they were (and still are) the material representations of fears, grief, and fulfilled wishes. Added together, the paintings and sculptures and popular artifacts created—or recreated—a world of magic and mystery for a jaded Old World culture. This was Breton's opinion at least (and Picasso's as well). The French fashion designer Elsa Schiaparelli seconded this view of Frida by designing an exotic garment—La Robe Madame Rivera—in her name. She was also given a bottle of the fragrance Shocking by the perfume division of Schiaparelli, a fragrance Frida used for the rest of her life. Some concluded it was to her liking for its dense floral scent; others thought that she used it to camouflage the smells of cigarette smoke and alcohol that permeated her skin and clothing. For all the elegance she exhibited, Frida was an addicted smoker and her drinking bouts did not lessen even after her debut in Paris.

The show opened on March 10, 1939, and the reviews were wonderful. Other artists, such as Wassily Kandinsky, attended the opening, and were so thrilled with her work that they embraced Frida and hovered around her with great enthusiasm. They gave her a lot of moral support, but few bought her paintings. The Louvre purchased one but, as for the artists, their excitement stopped before they pulled out their wallets. Already famous in his own right, and an admirer of Diego Rivera, Pablo Picasso made Frida a gift of earrings made of tiny hands, earrings that would appear in her later sketches and self-portraits. He did not, however, invest in her work. While Breton had written in his preface to the catalogue of her New York exhibit that "Frida Kahlo Rivera's work is a coloured ribbon around a bomb" (Breton 1967, cited in Alcántara and Egnolff 2005, 64, 149n), emphasizing her latent energy and sexuality underneath the disguise of her *Tehuana* costumes and rose-colored shawls, Frida remained an exotic discovery for the male Surrealist painters. Like Antonin Artaud's travels to the Mexican lands of the Tarahumaras in the 1930s to experiment with peyote and experience the total freedom of a life outside modern society, the European Surrealist painters viewed Kahlo's art, and Mexican culture in general, as mind-opening and filled with esoteric images. They were never acceptable objects of personal commerce; these, paradoxically, were for museums. Picasso visited the African continent to search for some primordial excitement the same way that Breton and Artaud traveled to Mexico City to refill their empty sources of inspiration. Long a domain of men, the European art scene did not really have a space for Frida except as an eccentric woman and the companion and muse of Diego Rivera. Diego's exploits during in student years in France were still legendary. When the International Surrealist Exhibition opened in 1940in Mexico City, there were only two Mexican artists represented: Frida Kahlo and Diego Rivera. Hardly a Surrealist, Rivera probably owed his part in the show to a personal favor by Breton. For her part, Kahlo did not identify herself as a Surrealist painter, but rather as an artist discovered by Surrealist painters. Many times she stated to friends and to critics alike that she had her own opinion on the matter: "They thought

I was a Surrealist, but I wasn't. I never painted dreams. I painted my own reality."

After enjoying great success in Paris, Frida returned home to Mexico City in the summer of 1939 to find that things remained tense between her and Diego. With Trotsky gone from the Blue House, and her father living alone, she decided to move back there. There are many theories about who proposed a divorce, but maybe Diego had heard of Frida's affairs in New York with Nikolas Muray and Isamu Noguchi, or maybe he had begun to be suspicious of the relationship between Trotsky and Kahlo. Or maybe he decided he was tired of their marriage. Whatever the impetus, the result was that Frida and Diego were legally divorced on November 6, 1939. Each already lived alone, Frida was painting up a storm, and Rivera had recently begun an affair with Hollywood star Paulette Goddard. Diego confessed—if his confession is to be believed since his ravenous appetite for invention rivaled his enormous appetites for painting and women—that he had never been faithful to any of his wives, not even his dear Frida, but that this was the type of man he was and he could not change for anyone. He feared that his wandering eye would harm her psychologically just as much as the accident had made her physical health more fragile. Yet he did not worry about this enough to stop the wedding. Married for just 10 years, he felt he needed the freedom to enjoy as many women as he wished without doing more damage to Frida (Herrera 1997, cited in Alcántara and Egnolff 2005, 67). These words sound more magnanimous than they were, and were received by Frida as a personal blow to the ego. She was devastated, since even living apart had been a painful time in her life and she did not want the independence Rivera seemed to prescribe for her. A divorce would just make things easier for Rivera: he could do whatever he pleased and, at least in public, claim he was no longer hurting his wife. Frida's drinking increased, in part because of the divorce and in part because of the return of her back pain. Encased in a corset to remedy her curving spine, she was photographed by Nikolas Muray without the glamour of the previous portraits. Frida's eyes are almost too large to look real, and are filled with signs of terror at how much she would have to endure. Frida begins to exhibit the wasted look of a woman both physically and emotionally drained.

Soon after the divorce, Frida painted one of her best-known works: *The Two Fridas* (1939). Quite large by her usual standards—about 68 × 68 inches—this double self-portrait could almost be an X-ray of Frida at a moment when her emotional and her physical pain competed equally to do her in. The swirling dark blue clouds behind two seated figures are not new to her canvases and have appeared in a few earlier works, but here they function to underscore the turbulence of the figures seated before them. Foreground and background merge to put the spectator on edge. Her earliest self-portraits were almost calm in comparison, framed by dark red or brown backgrounds that remained basically static. Now both nature and human nature combine to fill the scene with heartbreaking tension, confirmed by the visible hearts superimposed on each of the two Fridas and pumping their precious blood onto her skirt. The two halves of Frida—one in a *Tehuana* costume and one in a white formal dress—hold hands as if to combine their characteristics into one whole or to commiserate with the other's suffering. The Frida on the left is prim and proper, covered up to the neck with a starched white gown and carefully arranged hair. She has no jewelry but holds a small pair of scissors or pliers in one hand, an instrument used to stop the drip of blood into the whiteness of her skirt. Her heart has been cut open, and its chambers seem to be working to pump blood, as they must, even with this exposure. The slight curve of Frida's breast is visible underneath the heart, and the arteries that take the fluid to the rest of the body twine around her neck, bridging the space between the two halves of Frida and uniting them. The Frida on the right has her heart exposed, but it has not been sliced open. It too appears to continue functioning—both Fridas have the pink cheeks of a good, steady blood supply—and its tendrils (narrower than the arteries from her twin) encircle her arm. There is no dripping blood here, just a recycling of it over and over through the bodies of the two women. In her hand, the Frida on the right holds a tiny portrait. Shaped like a cameo, it shows a small figure of a boy in dark outline. Said to be Diego Rivera as a child—Frida reproduced the portrait from a small photograph of Diego—it is barely discernible due to its size. The eye of the viewer is drawn to the duplicate faces and the duplicated suffering of the two female figures, with the details of what might be the cause of their torment right in the middle of the scene but only visible upon careful scrutiny. The Frida on the right is wearing a long skirt that is almost a mustard color, like the earth below the two Fridas; she has a blue and yellow top almost exactly like one owned by Frida. The formal attire on the left and the indigenous dress on the right unite to give us a Frida Kahlo with a dual identity housed within a single life. Two bodies, two origins, two pieces of a puzzle come together to join the forces of nature in lamenting a love lost. The miniature Diego is a reminder of the miniscule amount of unfaithfulness that is needed to pierce the bosom of a woman and cause her infinite despair and heartbreak. Diego—sometimes called a force of nature by Frida herself—never left the picture, even after they were legally separated and removed from one another in geographical space. They had kept in touch even as they went their separate ways, and it did not take long for them to realize that they missed each other. Their divorce lasted about a year, and they were remarried on December 8, 1940, Diego's 54th birthday, in San Francisco where Diego had gone once again to work on a mural, this time for the Golden Gate International Exposition. As a symbol of their reunion, Frida ordered a special clock for her kitchen painted with the date of their remarriage. But as one nightmare was ending, another was about to begin for Frida.

Chapter 4

CAN'T LIVE WITH HIM, CAN'T LIVE WITHOUT HIM: REMARRIAGE, FRIDA STYLE

Legend has it that Frida agreed to remarry Diego on two conditions: the first was that she would contribute toward half the expenses of the running of the house using the profits from the sale of her paintings. The second was that she and Diego would refrain from any sexual relations. It seems that neither stipulation became a reality, however. Maybe the mutual attraction was so strong that they could not avoid physical contact, or maybe there was no need for her financial contribution in the eyes of an internationally famous artist like Rivera. It is not clear whether they truly made this agreement, but it makes a good story. Diego continued to work, still in demand even if fewer art commissions came in; and Frida produced some of her most recognizable portraits during the years following their reconciliation. This reunion of two strong and sometimes opposing forces opened the last decade and a half of Frida's life.

In any case, whether Frida made a lot of money or not, whether they reconciled in any real sense, or whether this was another piece of the myth, Diego had the murals for his commission from the Golden Gate show in San Francisco well under way when Frida called him with some bad news. Her health, always weak and precarious anyway, had suddenly taken a turn for the worse. Startled by the grave situation, Diego sent Frida directly to her old friend Dr. Leo Eloesser, who tried to figure out what might be done to alleviate her pain, or if indeed there would ever be an end to her suffering. After so many bouts of illness since her childhood, Frida was under no illusions about some complete cure. There was no way to rid her of the deformities of the scoliosis, of course, and her circulatory problems were only worsening with time and with age. If as a child she had felt self-conscious about her polio-stricken leg, as an adult the complications grew more serious and were no longer cosmetic or embarrassing, but life-threatening. Frida began to spend more and more time hospitalized, and she required more and more funds to pay the expenses related to her treatments, including drug therapy, doctors' consultations, and in the end amputations. Her paintings did sell, and she worked with energy between treatments to produce as many as she could and to find suitable investors in her artwork, but the reality was that Diego shouldered the majority of the expenses.

Her notebooks—now on display in the Blue House museum—reveal that between the expenses of building Anahuacalli, Diego's museum-like home designed to display his many pre-Columbian artifacts, and Frida's mounting medical care, even their combined income was not sufficient. As she recorded in her financial log, they often spent every cent of what they earned. It was lucky, of course, that she had been doing a large number of paintings; she started to sell these as fast as she could to Dr. Eloesser, to patrons in the United States and Mexico, and to old friends such as the Misrachi family, art dealers and book publishers of Jewish background who had helped Kahlo and her family in other times of need. Dolores Olmedo, a collector and philanthropist, bought a good number of Frida's paintings (and was given others as gifts). After Olmedo's death in 2002, her home was converted into a museum and gallery open to the public; it is filled with the valuable works of art she acquired over the years, especially the art of Diego and Frida. Her mansion, the Hacienda La Noria named for the waterwheel that was once located nearby, includes over 137 of Rivera's works, including his portrait of Olmedo herself. There are also 25 paintings of Frida Kahlo, and 37 drawings, sketches, and lithographs by Angelina Beloff (Rivera's first wife). Olmedo was the executor of the estates of both Diego and Frida, and her collection reflects her expertise in the field of fine art.

Paradoxically, as her health declined rapidly, Frida and Diego grew closer to one another. As Martha Zamora puts it, "parecieron encontrar placer simplemente en contemplarse mutuamente vivir" (they seemed to derive pleasure from simply contemplating one another's lives) (51). Not young any more, both Frida and Diego came to grips with the fact that neither was going to change. Once that had been faced, they could go on in relative peace. Besides, the mental anguish that Frida suffered during Diego's affairs did nothing to help her physical deterioration, and even Diego appeared to recognize that as she went through relapse after relapse. As he painted the mural for the lobby of the Mexico City Hotel del Prado, Diego found new inspiration in the company of Frida. He decided to include in his scene of a Sunday afternoon in the Alameda Park—a central city green space where rich and poor shared a stroll during their day of leisure—a portrait of Frida as a woman amid the crowd. She faces forward, wide-eyed and serene. Next to her, he painted himself as a young boy, chubby and baby-faced. She is the figure of the wise adult; he is the child that needs to hold on to her hand as the crowds press in. In Frida's hand he placed a Yin Yang symbol, the union of opposites and of equilibrium. It was a visible sign of their mutual truce, the declaration of peace that allowed them to join forces once again and be together. The past disappeared into the mists of time, or was consciously ignored. Diego's health was not the best, and Frida began to lose her battle with all of the diseases that had been her constant companions in the 33 short years of her life until then. Each used art as a force in the face of death. Diego tried to cheat death, to produce as much as possible before it closed the final chapter on his life. He often painted skeletons dressed in finery—*la Calaca*, or the popular female embodiment of death, since the word is feminine in Spanish—amid bustling city life, or as a sidekick to Frida. Death was part of every day; it became a force that they would eventually have to confront. Why wish it invisible? That would be a denial that Mexican popular culture does not admit. If Diego worked incessantly to fill the days and years with paintings and murals, Frida painted to stave off the end that, as she confessed to everyone, terrified her even as she recognized its face next to her own. The closer that final moment came, the wider her eyes became in her last photos. It was as if she actually saw a figure coming to take her away. All jokes aside—and Mexican culture is full of lyrics with mischievous and taunting refrains, melodies, and little rhymes about death—Frida had begun to take her life more seriously.

With her physical body in decline, Frida paradoxically enjoyed one of the most prolific and celebrated periods of artistic creation in her life. A series of self-portraits initiated after *The Two Fridas* reveals an adult woman with a very serious gaze who looks out at the world knowingly. She is no longer a little girl, no longer the playful Frida who taunted Diego on the scaffold or confronted his women on the street. There were no more secrets for her, no illusions, and she took this in stride as she reunited with her two loves—Diego Rivera and painting. The decade of the 1940s was filled with introspection for Frida, with a sense of urgency, and her eyes were wide open when it came to Diego and his true character. He was a chaser of women, he would come and go from country to country, and he would also support her work with his long-time friends and gallery owners. He was a sum total of numerous opposites, not too different from the Yin Yang the painted Frida held in her hand in his hotel mural. He could decide to stay with her in the Blue House, or to be without her in his studio in San Angel or his house in Coyoacán; it no longer mattered to her. Frida had made her own decision to return to the one place she had always called home—the Blue House. She never left that protective environment again, even as Diego came and went. Little by little, the home inherited from her parents—she was the only daughter to return there to live—was transformed into Frida's house. It took on all the characteristics of whimsy and fantasy that had been Frida's trademarks.

Once more confined periodically to sedentary life, and submitting to operations in New York and California, Frida turned an obstacle into an opportunity. Her face and her emotional state—a curious mixture of relief at being reunited with Diego and anxiety about her illness—became central to her vision of life, particularly her own. The decade of the 1940s is documented through her countenance reflected in the mirror. Maybe looking at this surface was a way to make sure she was still there and visible to others, not fading away into invisibility. Or maybe it was a way to check on the daily changes in her features as pain ebbed and flowed. Whatever the cause, Frida was never far from a mirror and she became obsessed with them.

In addition to herself, in the 1940s Frida turned out portraits of Natasha Gelman, the wife of Russian-born film producer Jacques Gelman, an avid collector of Mexican art and friend of the Riveras. She also painted small portraits of Eduardo Morillo Safa and his wife Lupe, both friends since adolescence. Besides the parents, Frida also did paintings of their children and other relatives of the family, especially the grandparents. Her interest in family lineage, and in extended family members, may have encouraged this series of portraits. Then again, it could merely have been the personal connection between them, or the idea that her pleasure in painting them also brought reimbursement. The poignancy of the children's faces close-up is not lost on the viewer, since the early dream of having her own children had long disappeared as she and Diego declared a truce and never addressed that issue again. One could just imagine Frida having the Morillo Safa son and daughter sit in her studio in the Blue House, posed with clean clothing and ribbons and neatly-combed hair—just as she had tried to sit still for her father's photographic portraits when she was their age. Frida painted close-up portraits of them, but they remained still for the paintbrush as she had to learn to do for her father's camera. Despite all these small commissions and projects, however, Frida spent much of her time looking at the details of a face in crisis—her own. Some of her portraits were commissioned by buyers as famous and influential as the United States industrial magnate

Seymour Firestone, but others were purchased after she had completed them for herself.

Between 1940 and 1950, Frida produced over 18 self-portraits depicting extreme close-ups of her face and shoulders. No single portrait is very large and every inch of each is filled with color, detail, and a background of nature that frames her face. The earlier examples of this genre—paintings of the first few years of the 1940s—surround her serious countenance with dark green foliage, pink or red ribbons, small monkeys, crowns of tropical flowers, leaves, trees, parrots, sparrows, stone beads, and elaborate hair ornaments. She chose most frequently to show her hair pinned up in braids wound around her head in intricate shapes, sometimes covered with a traditional black lace *mantilla* or head scarf, and other times crowned with butterflies and flower blossoms. These styles echo the indigenous women's penchant for long hair, but they also are evidence of Frida's increasing attention to the details of her body as she began to feel it slip away in bits and pieces. The more the doctors removed, the more the hair swirls around her face; the more her bones disintegrated, the more she pinned ribbons and bows to her clothing and covered her fingers with rings. The jewelry had been a *Vogue* magazine style note when she accompanied Muray to New York and Paris; in the 1940s, her jewelry made sure people looked at her, and that she would not fade away. Except for the painting entitled *Self-portrait with Short Hair,* where she appears dressed in a man's suit, with scissors in hand and locks of hair all around her, all of the other examples of the period show her decorated with colorful items and surrounded by flora and fauna. A creature of the natural world, Frida vitalized her own face by placing it amid living plants and animals that might add energy to her ebbing life.

In the 1940 self-portrait dedicated to Firestone and his daughters, purchased as a pair with a self-portrait of Diego done by him, her expression is somber and the details of her simple white linen blouse, shell necklace, and elaborate head covering create a sober picture. It is more formal than pleasant. The background color is a pale yellow, and nothing seems vibrant or lively. Frida's face is dark, her hair is even darker, and her nose appears to cast a shadow across her cheek. It could be the point of view—the artist looking in a tilted mirror—but the shadow haunts her cheek like a ghost. Frida is never seen smiling in any of her previous self-portraits, but here she looks almost angry, or maybe it is the resignation she began to feel toward her illnesses that casts a shadow across her face. Her cheeks do not look naturally pink, but are rather painted with makeup as an antidote to her lack of color and vibrancy, a hedge against the pallor of death. There are lines and wrinkles under her eyes, evidence of sleepless nights and constant pain. Even her eyes are darker in color than usual here. Her signature eyebrows crown her forehead with darkness and her slight moustache is visible right over painted lips. All of the elements are present, and hers is a recognizable face, but Frida has aged and is visibly less carefree and challenging than before. This is a formal portrait, as the dedication on the curling piece of paper on the wall behind her indicates, and there is no joy evident in any aspect of it. Maybe it was the money paid for it that lessened the joy, but maybe the sorrow emanated from inside the face itself and not from the events imposed on it.

The same affect holds true for two other self-portraits of the same year, the first painted for Nathan Wedeen (now held in a private collection) and the second dedicated to her dear friend Dr. Leo Eloesser. All three of these paintings show Frida looking slightly at an angle to the viewer, one to her left and the other two slightly toward her right. They also share a melancholy, gloomy, grave tone, even if the colors of the background and of her face are slightly more lustrous and intense in the second two than in the Firestone portrait. But the pinkish tone and the shine could just as well be fever as signs of life. Frida's face is thin and heavily rouged; her flesh looks too rosy to be natural and healthy. Health was no longer a part of her life, so it had to be shown artificially. Her dark eyes look to one side, most likely owing to the mirror she used to observe as she painted, and there is no expression on her features. Her lips are together, her eyebrows float like birds' wings over her dark eyes, and her increasingly ornate hairdo creates a halo around this sad face. The more the hair is elevated above the level of her eyes, the more attention is drawn away from the stark look they hold. The thinness of her jaw line is offset by the sheer amount of ribbons and bows, flowers and leaves, serapes and colorful garments, which appear on every side of her. Reds and greens predominate, so much so that when the thorns surrounding her long, thin neck in place of the usual piece of jewelry prick her skin, the red of her blood blends in with the rest of the scarlet tones. Fulang Chang, a pet monkey she had in the Blue House and one of several little animals such as the fawn *Granizo* (Hail) that kept her company, wraps his arm around her in the portrait for Nathan Wedeen. His bright eyes seem to mirror hers as they gaze straight ahead.

The necklace of thorns is a prelude to other portraits that are filled with pain and suffering, although Frida used indirect ways of showing that. She does not shed a tear—at least not yet—but her whole face reflects her struggle with life. In *Autorretrato con collar de espinas y colibrí* (Self-portrait with thorn necklace and hummingbird), also painted in 1940, Frida continued to portray the sacrificial blood of an inner pain in the red drops spilling down her neck. Ever since *The Two Fridas*, trickling blood is part of all her self-portraits. But she added a hummingbird to this scene, a talisman for those in search of true love and a symbol of accomplishing what seems impossible. Hummingbirds represent finding joy in the most difficult circumstances. In alternative medicine—something near to Frida and her surroundings in Coyoacán—the hummingbird is the symbol of natural cures to be found in flowers and seeds. Here, however, this tiny fluttering creature is still and unmoving, strung around her neck like a weight to bear. In her hair are lacy white butterflies poised and paralyzed, and on her right shoulder Fulang Chang returns, scratching the dead twigs of the necklace. On Frida's left shoulder a black cat—a much more sinister talisman or omen than the hummingbird—puts a paw stealthily on her white dress. The cat's green eyes and Frida's dark brown ones stare straight ahead, as if they could see us looking at them. This time, Frida wears no jewelry but the thorns, and her standard decorative clothing has been exchanged for a simple white cotton blouse or dress. The hair on her face is more prominent, her ears are uncharacteristically bare of decoration, and the three sets of eyes—the cat, the monkey, and Frida's—reflect little emotion. They are capable of seeing outward but reveal nothing of the inside of the living being. Frida has simultaneously shut herself off and made us look at her.

Two self-portraits painted in 1941—for Natasha and Juan Gelman (the art collector, cinema producer, and an old friend of Frida and Diego), the first from a point of view much further away, and the second from much closer up then before—keep the general pose of the previous paintings but show fading light and fading colors. *Autorretrato con trenza* (Self-portrait with Braid) has a very muted background for an equally muted skin tone. The once-green leaves of the foliage have turned gray and brown, and there is a grayish tinge to nature and to her flesh. There is no doubt that this is Frida, for we see her familiar hair and pink cloth twined through it. But the energy once filling her eyes has disappeared and the scene feels flat. The close-up portrait entitled *Autorretrato con fondo café* (Self-portrait with brown background) could be no more explicit about the mood—gray and brown frame a face whose details are easy to detect. The grain of the canvas—Frida by then had moved up from boards to true canvas—shows through, and the brushstrokes used to paint her cheeks and even the wisps of her sideburns untucked from the hairdo are clear. This Frida is about the particulars—the whites of the eyes, the deep furrow under the nose, each hair of the brow, the fuzz along the chin. Unlike the other, more typical self-portrait, this one asks for a closer inspection. It doesn't allow for distraction from the face to the background, and it forces one to look at the details. Alongside her head, Frida painted her name in very large letters (not standard for her), and she dated the painting with Roman numerals MCMXLI (also not her usual style). It would be easy to categorize her 18 works of the 1940s and 1950s as "self-portraits" without taking account of what distinguishes each from the others. But this 1941 portrait would contradict that, since it focuses on the head and neck, and suggests a very earthy silhouette in the colors of Mexican clay and sand. The roses and pinks have all but evaporated.

Frida called her 1941 portrait *Autorretrato con Bonito* (Self-portrait with Pretty Bird) a portrait of her mourning for her father. He had recently died after suffering a heart attack. He was 69 years old, young according to contemporary standards. Epilepsy had plagued him his entire life, and he and Frida had always shared a view of life conditioned by their physical ailments. Frida confessed to her friends and to Dr. Eloesser that this event saddened her indescribably. She had returned from the United States when her mother died, but at that time confessed to the chasm that had separated them emotionally. Now the situation was much more dramatic for her. Of her father, Frida wrote in her diary: "although he was a sick man he was an immense example to me of tenderness, of work.. and above all of understanding for all my problems." His death had a great impact on her since she lost the human being closest to her in temperament, and the man whose companion she had been during his travels for the government when she had assisted with his camera equipment. Having warned Diego of Frida's headstrong manner, Guillermo had revealed his intimate knowledge of her strengths and weaknesses, and perhaps even his own identification with them. Now no one was left to be on her side. She and Diego were truly alone (except for friends and acquaintances in the art world).

Eleven years after he died and only two years before her death, Frida painted her *Portrait of Don Guillermo Kahlo,* using the elegant and formal title of a man to be respected and revered. "Don" is more than just Mr., for it hints at deference and admiration. His daughter's use of the honorific name unveils the importance of this figure in her life. As she herself was about to pass from it, he surfaced as the subject of a portrait that must be done before it was too late, and both of them were gone. He had always been the man behind the camera to document his daughter's life; now she had one last portrait to do to assure the survival of his. The inscribed scroll below the painting reads: "Pinté a mi padre Wilhelm Kahlo; de origen húngaro alemán; artista fotógrafo de profesión; de carácter generoso inteligente y fino valiente porque padeció durante sesenta años epilepsia, pero jamás dejó de trabajar y luchó contra Hitler, con admiración, su hija, Frida Kahlo" (I painted my father Wilhelm Kahlo, Hungarian German by birth, photographic artist by profession, generous, intelligent, and refined by nature, brave because for sixty years he suffered from epilepsy but he never stopped working, he fought against Hitler, with admiration, his daughter Frida Kahlo). Even as her own self-portraits lose some of their liveliness and as her image fades into paleness, her father leaps right off the canvas with intensity and color. She has brought him back to life with her detailed brush strokes and careful re-creation.

All of the elements of this painting evoke the aspects she describes in the banner: he looks sedate, professional, steady, and calm. Returning to the past and calling him once again by the German version of his name, Wilhelm, and so revisiting his European origins and therefore her own, Frida set her father against a mottled, swirling backdrop. Seated in the formal manner of her own photographic portraits, Don Wilhelm is dressed in a three-piece suit, white shirt with stiff collar, and red tie. The buttons and handkerchief in his pocket not only reflect his actual form of dress during his working days, but also attest to her interest in capturing every bit of her memories of him. She recalls her father in his younger days as a man with a dark moustache and dark, thick hair. His light blue eyes—which she commented on over many years, especially in contrast to her own brown eyes—shine with light and stare off into the distance. She captured him down to the last nuance: his eyebrows so like hers, his long ears, the cleft in his chin. And true to the caption underneath, Frida placed his camera right next to him, since his ethnic origin, his valiant spirit, and his professional work stand out as his three most distinguishing characteristics. That he was in Mexico already as an immigrant long before Hitler came to power need not intrude on the notion that, for Frida at least, his opposition to Hitler was another facet of his myth that she wished to keep alive. Guillermo was as much a product of his adoring daughter as Diego was of his own fan club.

Frida's own mourning portrait as she contemplates her own face after her father's death—a painting whose current location is now unknown—displays another moment in her physical and emotional decline related to her own health. She may have a parrot (the Pretty Bird of the painting's title) on her shoulder, and a Monarch butterfly may flit around behind her, but she is sedate and downcast. A year later, in *Autorretrato con chango y loro* (Self-portrait with monkey and parrot), Frida repeats the same cast of characters and again looks stern. Nature still surrounds her, but certain elements of life have started to disappear, leaving her alone with the pets. Huge dried palms woven into mourning patterns for Christian celebrations of death and resurrection at Easter time fill the canvas, spilling onto her shoulders and into the tiny grasp of Fulang Chang. The parrot is almost too big to look real (or to fly), and Frida's darkened skin becomes one with the deep gold of the flat background and the palm fronds. From here to *Pensando en la muerte* (Thinking about Death), a year later in 1943, is a short leap.

Just over ten years before her own death, only two since her father's, and with sickness increasingly intruding into the hours of each day, Frida began to place herself among the departed more than the living, at least in her art. She discovered the Eastern notion of the third eye in the middle of the forehead as a symbol of a higher plane of reality, and converted it into her own shorthand for representing her thoughts. These thoughts increasingly turned to people she had lost, memories of family members, and the notion of death itself as part of life. Among these tiny circles opening just over her eyebrows and centered in both placement and consciousness are the skull and crossbones, followed by miniatures of Diego (himself with a third eye). Perhaps strangely and paradoxically, the face containing the thoughts of death looks less agonized and anguished than in the previous couple of portraits. The painted Frida has regained the natural color of her face and neck, and her hair is back to a normal length and style. She is surrounded by greenery and not dead branches, there is no oozing blood, and she once again wears a patterned native dress in reds and golds. It is doubtful that she is returning to a former state of joy or stasis; rather, she seems to have found a way to externalize her grief and cast it onto the canvas. Painting always held a therapeutic power for her ever since her accident, and the addition of a new element such as the third eye may have been an encouraging factor in her self-analysis through art. Not having to hold tragedy inside, but molding it into the shape of a death's head, made her morbid thoughts more visible, more universal perhaps, and the objects of compassion. One could always empathize with someone who had lost a parent, suffered an operation, been divorced, or been chronically ill. Mexican plants and animals, strikingly colored ornaments and ribbons, and women in *Tehuana* outfits were less identified with as items shared by many than the critical moments of life. Frida's losses and her death images began to signal the end of her days, but for others, they also opened up a whole new sense of identification with her.

Her 1943 *Diego en mi pensamiento* (Diego in My Thoughts) and the 1949 *Diego y yo* (Diego and I) form two sides of one coin related to the last third of Frida's works during this decade, and her turn to imagery related to internal, perhaps even subconscious, fears. Again part of the collection of paintings owned by the Gelmans, *Diego in My Thoughts* has become one of Kahlo's most identifiable self-portraits. Just as *The Two Fridas* split a single personality in half to lay bare the hidden suffering, so this painting brings to light a beautifully wrapped package—Frida—inhabited by dark thoughts. Maybe André Breton had been right about her—Frida was indeed a ribbon around a bomb. The overwhelming lace shawl, fringed with lavender satin ribbon and striped flowing material, covers all of Frida but her face. The neck is not visible, and whatever other garments she might have on do not matter. What calls attention to her features, and to the tiny image of Diego that fills her forehead, only to be stopped by the forest of her eyebrows, is the starched oval circle of lace that encloses her like the medieval wimple hid the shaved head of the nun. This type of cloth usually covered the head, neck, and chin, and would keep a woman's hair from view. A wimple might be linen or cotton or made of another elaborately starched fabric, creased and folded, even supported on a wire or wicker frame. This is not true of Frida's head covering, which glistens with satin sheen around the edges, is covered with embroidered white flowers, and allows the front portion of her hairline to show through. It is crowned with a bouquet of wild flowers—including white and yellow daisies, deep pink bougainvilleas, and green fronds—from which tiny tendrils emerge to fill the canvas and reach to its edges and even beyond. There are thin roots of life that emerge from the petals to spray across the portrait in search of light or water or sustenance. These diminutive vines connect Frida's face to the world, and they nurture her thoughts like the one of Diego visible above her eyes. Like the spiritual eye she read about in her collection of volumes on healing and medicine—neither excluded the potential power of the other—Diego might have represented for her the so-called dormant organ (the pineal gland) that could be awakened to enable telepathic communication between kindred spirits. If Rivera had painted her in his Mexico City hotel mural as a woman holding the balance of the universe in her hands—in the black and white Yin Yang globe she caresses between long fingers—then Frida dived into the same spiritual reservoir for support in her time of crisis.

Frida echoed this portrait in a close-up of her face that she called *Autorretrato con medallón* (Self-portrait with medallion) in 1948, in which there is a similar halo of crimped lace around her face and a cascade of flowers embroidered on the shawl that emerges from it. Yet, aside from the medallion of the title, Frida added another new component: a tear spilling out of each eye. Her emotions are cautiously contained, her lips pursed, but something inside begs to be let out. It emerges at the moment of portraiture as the artist looks with care at her own face, making it less a study and more the chance to capture the human spirit. The beauty of the detailed fabric covers the entire surface of the Masonite board, and the gold medallion with pearls and a dove is carefully rendered to reflect its artistry. Yet the real work of art is the emotion that trickles, almost unnoticed, from her eyes. Two tears encapsulate and encompass an entire life.

While there was no third eye in this 1948 self-portrait, in *Diego and I* Frida returned to the theme of the couple and to her fascination with the mystical evocation of Diego (and another eye visible on his forehead) as something she carried with her always. Like the image of her father that she created in loving detail a decade after his death, Frida has been haunted by thoughts of Diego both throughout their years together and in their lives apart. Even if they were separated geographically, her portrait shows that she carried him with her. The glycerine-like tears from the previous year's painting have multiplied from two to three; yet Frida's eyes, as well as Diego's eyes and the third eye he exhibits all remain unblinking. As her dark hair swirls in concentric circles around her throat, protecting it and obliterating it from view at the same time, nothing interrupts the steady gaze of the woman in the painting. She seemed to take sustenance from this presence in her subconscious, and wrote in her diary, "Diego es mi padre, Diego es mi creador, Diego es mi fin y mi principio, yo soy de Diego, Diego es mío. Pero no. No. Diego no es de Frida, Diego es de él" (Diego is my father, Diego is my creator, Diego is my end and my beginning, I belong to Diego, Diego is mine. But no. No. Diego does not belong to Frida, Diego belongs to himself). Switching from first person (I) to third person (Frida) as she writes about her relationship with this force of nature, Frida analyzes the situation as she describes it. First, she links them inextricably as soul mates (belonging to one another), then she finds this untrue. She says no twice, and moves on to distance herself from both of them—Frida and Diego, not he and I—and to deny the possibility that either could actually "belong" in any sense of possession to the other. Closeness aside, Diego could never be captured by even the strongest power of the will, and Frida could carry him inside her but he would always be just a bit too independent and self-sufficient to be her possession. No one could have been closer to him, but there would always be a space where she could not enter. When interviewed after their remarriage, each of them vowed that their spirits would always remain united. Yet that new relationship had been a renegotiation of both the good and the bad of their previous years. It was really a turning point, a time to take stock of what had gone before, and a conscious decision that despite the daily challenges with one another, they were somehow destined to be together. Close friends vouched for their being inseparable, and that the reports of preconditions for remarriage were untrue.

Before she turned to several self-portraits that uncovered the real or symbolic scars on the surface of her body, Frida found one more way to represent the relationship between herself and Diego. Her *Retrato doble Diego y yo* (Double portrait Diego and I) of 1944 (actually two similar portraits, one of which has disappeared, that were meant to be a pair) combined Frida's interest in popular arts and crafts and her talent at portraiture. The frame is very small, a mere 2½ inches by four inches, and is covered with seashells brought from the region of Veracruz on the gulf coast. The colors are opalescent white and peach as the small shells are split, sliced, and glued onto a wooden frame that looks something like a scroll or a tiny harp. Inside the center space is the double portrait, with half of Frida's face on the right juxtaposed with half of Diego's face on the left. He is pale and she is dark, he is slightly feminized in this diminutive version of his large head, but she retains her distinctive features. Their noses and mouths meet and seem to morph into each other, while their eyes are dissimilar. Diego is shown with the large and popping eyes he had in real life; Frida's brown eyes recede into the portrait and almost disappear among the painted shells, driftwood, half moon, tubers, and vines she adds to weave an entire scene together and connect it to the oceanic artifacts of the frame. There are not two heads but one, not two individuals but a single entity amid the flotsam of the gulf seas. Diego, Frida, seashells, sand and surf: all add up to a single unit that is Mexico and with which they are one and inseparable.

The reconciliation of Frida and Diego on a personal level did not mean that her physical obstacles had been surmounted, however. As she hastened to finish the portraits that sold quickly to old friends such as the engineer Eduardo Morillo Safa, who had met Frida during her short time at the *Prepa*, travelers from abroad would arrive in Mexico City and hear of the artist who had undergone so many surgical interventions, so many experimental treatments, and who continued to paint despite these setbacks. The market for her art grew in the mid-1940s; many of her paintings in this period were done between hospitalizations, or during the visits of foreigners, and therefore were never completed. But those works Frida did manage to finish gained her a deserved reputation as an avant-garde painter. In their themes, and in the unexpected and sometimes fairly shocking treatments of those themes, she singlehandedly established the boundaries of women's art in Mexico among vivid colors, still lifes of local fruits and vegetables, and revealing self-portraits. These paintings were not only self-portraits in the ordinary sense of a bust encircled by natural elements, but also included fragments of the human body, obsessions kept inside, and established a link between physical or material life and the life of the mind. Her disintegrating and broken spinal column inspired three fascinating and quite unorthodox portraits of her pain: *La columna rota* (The Broken Column, 1944), part of the collection belonging to Dolores Olmedo; the surgical brace and bleeding torso of her double self-portrait *Arbol de la esperanza mantente firme* (Tree of Hope Remain Strong, 1946); and the personification of her pain as a hunted animal in a forest filled with the arrows of those out to hurt or destroy her in *La venadita o El venadito herido* (The Wounded Deer or the Wounded Doe, 1946).

These three works of art are moving evidence of her struggle to maintain some notion of a normal life even as her body seemed to be collapsing and falling to pieces. The first follows on the heels of her father's death by only a couple of years, and it shows on canvas what had happened to her in the flesh. With the calcium of her spinal column deteriorating by the day, Frida entered the *Hospital Inglés* (English Hospital) in Mexico City, an institution renowned for its cutting edge treatment of even the most difficult diseases, to receive a bone graft that everyone hoped would fortify her weakening vertebrae. There are tender photographs of Diego visiting Frida in the hospital, and one of them holding onto each other for dear life and kissing passionately even as she was immobilized in bed once again. The graft would never be as successful as both the Riveras and their physicians hoped, but Frida never gave up on procedures that held still a tiny sliver of optimism for a better quality of life. The painting of her torso shows her face no longer impassive but filled with tears. There are not two or three drops but oceans of salty tears covering her cheeks and dribbling down her chin. What most startles is that her torso has been cracked open—a vestige of Frida's studies of drawing and biology during her *Prepa* days in the hope of becoming a doctor—to reveal an architectural column splintered and in large fragments. The cracks along its surface are in part the fluting of the design and in part ruptures that will eventually cause it to fall. This is not a house built on solid foundations; Frida's body is a structure just on the verge of crumbling. The white straps encircling her shoulders and ribs do not seem to be strong enough or numerous enough to keep that column from falling into dust. Even the numerous tacks—close to two-dozen metal nails are scattered from her shoulders to the white sheet that covers her lower body—can't hold things together. Bloodied and falling to the ground, they do not keep the pieces of her failing body in place. The flesh of her abdomen is opened to show the faulty foundation on which the external body relies, and it leaves her two arms almost floating in mid-air, helpless to do anything but grasp at the sheet that is in danger of slipping to the ground and leaving her totally naked.

The remaining flesh of her torso is unblemished on the surface, but the tragedy just beneath it is now there for all to see.

The second painting, the elusive tree of hope that she wished to survive, shows Frida on the edge of a precipice clutching a steel corset that would be her life vest after the operation. Like a shipwrecked passenger, the portrait shows Frida holding onto this apparatus for dear life, even as she peers into the abyss. Behind the fully dressed version of herself holding the corset, and a banner that tells us the reason she painted this was her immobility after the operation on her spine, appears her own body lying motionless on a hospital gurney, its back gashed open and dripping blood. This does not look like the small, dried blood of the necklace of thorns that the hummingbird hangs near; it looks like a red and raw liquid that means life is slipping away as it leaves her inert body. One Frida faces us and one lies facing scenery split into two: on the left is a bloody sun in an angry-looking sky presiding over a scorched earth; on the right is the complementary other half of a darkened sky barely lit by a full moon that does not have enough light to brighten the dark gray parched earth. There is no water, there is no life. Days come and go, sun and moon appear and disappear. Frida remains, like the tree of hope. But for how long can she stave off the end?

The last years of the 1940s and the transition into a new decade held increasing recognition for Frida's talent as an artist and simultaneously a growing number of hospital stays. She spent nine months under treatment in the latter part of 1949 and early 1950, during which she lost a third of her right leg—from the foot almost to the knee and underwent psychiatric treatment by Dr. Ramón Parres (Zamora 1987, 132). A few of the internments might have been spurred by her depression, something noted by her close friends and in her own diary, and by rumored suicide attempts. Versions of her medical stays vary from the morbid to the lively, but the one true factor is that the deaths of several servants in her employ, and the stories of rampant viral problems in the hospital itself, left Frida contemplating the end of life more than any other topic. This translated into a few paintings that she worked on between 1949 and 1950, at least one of which was never completed. All of them reflected her frame of mind and each contributed a piece to the puzzle of her total condition, both mental and physical. Suffering from chronic pain, Frida even found some solace in her long hospital stays and the attention she was paid by the medical staff and others during these times. Photographs from 1950 show her either being attended by nurses and physicians while lying in her bed, or surrounded by servants as she paints. Art and medicine are both constant companions.

In 1949, two paintings stand out as representative of her bouts with disease and treatment: *El abrazo de amor de El universo, La tierra (México) yo, Diego y el señor Xólotl* (The Love Embrace of the Universe, Earth (Mexico), Me, Diego, and Mr. Xólotl). This painting was not labeled, but Frida spoke this title to all those who visited her. As Frida wrote in her diary, "Mi pintura lleva el mensaje del dolor" (My paintings carry the message of pain) (Zamora 1987, 353); if this was true, she was also consoled by all of her natural surroundings as she suffered. From the greatest to the smallest element, the world comes to her rescue at her time of need in this scene, in which Frida and Diego are dwarfed and shown as just two among the many, many components of life on earth. Day and night, sun and moon, earth and sky, air and water, dry cactus and green foliage, all of the opposites imaginable are unified and held in the loving arms of the universe. One arm is brown and one is white, the forces holding them close and encircling Diego and Frida have masks but they are obviously female. Frida's tiny *esquintle* dog—a modern remnant of the Aztec Chihuahuas fattened up for the dinner table—Mr. Xólotl cowers to one side, curled up amid the leaves and vines, alone but accompanied by the Baroque world in which they all live. There are not fewer elements in her world as Frida begins to lose the battle with her body, but more. She populated her canvases with greater quantities of living things, as life couldn't always be counted on any more. The one power that survived it all was what she titled the entire work: the embrace of love. Frida had always seemed to see love as relative—the ambiguous love between her parents, the strained love of mother and daughter, the competitive love for and from Diego, the undying love of Nikolas Muray and Isamu Noguchi—but somehow it all came together as the universe scooped up its fragments and made them into a whole.

In 1949, Frida began a painting as she began her recovery from the spinal operations in the English Hospital. In 1950, when she was released, it still had not been finished, but it now sits on an easel in the Blue House museum as evidence of her use of art as therapy. *Mi familia* (My family), sketched out but not completed, was Frida's vision of her life, a mere four years before her death, spread out before her. She places herself at center, along the bottom of the frame, surrounded by her sisters, nieces, and nephews. Above their generation are her parents, Guillermo and Matilde. At the top of the small canvas—once again only about 15 by 20 inches—appear her two sets of grandparents. The two previous generations before Kahlo herself float in a cloud, perhaps signaling their no longer being on earth or their nebulous existence in her memory. She paints her grandmothers and mother as serene, serious women dressed in formal attire; her grandfathers are equally posed as official subjects of an official document. Frida and her sisters are recognizable, and they stand side-by-side, all in dark brown. Frida's *Tehuana* outfit is visible, but the bright red and gold of the cloth is darkened, making her blend in among them all. What floats above her slightly to the left is more telling—the same fetus she drew during her stay in the Henry Ford Hospital in Detroit, and the same fetus that seemed to accompany her throughout her life with Diego. The tiny body hovers between her and her parents, a constant reminder of loss. This self-portrait embedded within a family history gives Frida's face a context, a past and a present. Any questions she might have been forming about her own survival and her legacy may have been the catalyst for looking at her own face amid similar ones.

As the decade of the 1950s dawned, Frida welcomed the New Year in from her bed. Lucky to be alive, yet disheartened by what it took for that to happen, Frida turned to painting the portraits of the men who had been her allies in the fight against death, her doctors. In addition to her long-time friend Dr. Leo Eloesser, Dr. Juan Farrill was added to the pantheon of her cherished saviors. Dr. Farrill was the one who performed the spinal graft and the one who she said gave her back the joy of living. In 1951, when she returned to the Blue House, Frida painted herself alongside a painted portrait of Dr. Farrill as a personal form of payment for his care. She is seated in a wheelchair, and in her hands are many brushes; her palette is her heart. As always, Frida painted with every organ of her body and not just her eyes and hands; she made this obvious to all in *Autorretrato con el Dr. Juan Farrill* (Self-portrait with Dr. Juan Farrill, 1951). Even without the use of her legs and back, she turned to the source of her treatment to pay her respects and give homage to his work. His face on the canvas is truly a result of her blood and tears.

Chapter 5

THE COMPANY OF WOMEN AND THE DIARY'S LAST ENTRY

Seven spinal operations in the span of two years (1950 1951) spurred on hundreds of tender messages sent back and forth between Frida and Diego as she sank lower into each consecutive stage of her illness and he spent more time working. They left one another torn-off sheets of paper filled with pen-and-ink sketches of flowers, wrapped around tidbits of sweets and food, and promises of hundreds of kisses when she awakened. He told her he was sleeping at the studio; she responded that wherever he was comfortable that was fine with her. Taking on commission after commission, Diego worked day and night to pay the light bills and the other costs of running their houses, as well as additional medical expenses for her treatment. He wasn't the best administrator of their funds and even had to exchange paintings for electricity when his bill was overdue. Frida had always been the accountant, so her decline meant less management of these things than before. Diego was more interested in social events, friends, and keeping up appearances as a wild and inspired artist.

His kind words for his sick little girl—*mi niña Frida* or *Fisita* or *Friducha*—and her insistent remonstrations for his working too hard are part of the collection of gentle, loving notes between them. Sometimes they were left on her nightstand as she slept, other times they were on the counter for him in the morning. These passing words were supplemented by visits from Arturo García Bustos, one of her students among *Los Fridos*, her protégés who carried on their work after spending years at her side in the studio and honoring her with flowers on Mother's Day. That these artists adopted her as both mentor and a maternal figure caused Frida some displeasure. Frida did not like the reminder of her lack of children, and she balked at the young men playing a role other than as students of her popular painting techniques. Their visits became reminders of the world outside that she was no longer part of as frequently as she would have liked, and of her own solitude with the only one she could baby—Diego. Since Frida was hardly a typical instructor for *Los Fridos*, their lessons were learned on site in *cantinas* (popular bars) and other gathering places around the Blue House. They painted murals on the walls of several of these drinking establishments and even held parties right there to celebrate the completion of their work. Even if she was not pleased by their consideration of her as a maternal figure, Frida enjoyed the company of these young men and the fact that they would pay to study with her. It made her feel equal to other artists who had studios and gave lessons, and it gave her an audience not dependent on Diego and his fellow artists.

As a promoter of a native kind of art—both in style and in content—Frida actually fulfilled what Rivera and the other post-Revolutionary muralists such as Siqueiros had always advocated. Their insistence on an indigenous American style instead of a mere copy of European models ended up influencing the hybrid forms they used. The color palette of Mexican artists reflected the reds, deep pinks, ochres, and dramatic blues of the landscape while using those tones to frame subjects related to independence, freedom from empire, and democratic values for the masses. But while they had worked on a larger scale and in more public venues, Frida paved the way for women to express themselves from the inside out and in more intimate circumstances. Like the diary that functioned as a record of her thoughts and worries, Frida's small canvases were fragments of an internal life that complemented the outer politics of the Mexican men and women portrayed by Rivera, Orozco, and Siqueiros. When asked about Frida's paintings, and even in unsolicited opinions for journalists and art critics, Rivera always stressed her masterful self-portraits. No one did them as well as she did in his opinion, and that statement was so universal that it must contain at least a grain of truth. Frida would leave her imprint on *Los Fridos*, who carried on her tradition and style of painting.

During the first part of the 1950s, Isolda and Antonio, the children of her sister Cristina, saw their Aunt Frida several times a week and, by all accounts, she treated them kindly until her pain became overwhelming and she could no longer tolerate their noise and youthful enthusiasm. Isolda recalls her delight at visiting with her aunt, but her fear of Frida's dying at any minute. The risk of her not making it through the next round of surgery was always present despite the smiling face put on by all. When Isolda writes of her ever-present anxiety she is already an adult, but Frida's delicate situation must have made a lasting impression on her as a young woman. Despite her aunt's advice to joke about death while she was spirited and full of life, Isolda felt the sadness of her final illness. Isolda writes, "Lo más triste que puedo recordar de esos años de mi vida, es el día de la muerte de Frida. Siempre ese riesgo estuvo latente en cada cirugía a la cual fue sometida. Naturalmente, siempre estábamos temiéndolo. Durante cada nueva convalecencia creímos que no superaría la prueba" (Isolda P. Kahlo 2004, 37). (The saddest thing I remember about that time of my life was the day that Frida died. That risk was always present with each surgery she went through. Naturally, we were always afraid of that. During each subsequent convalescence, we believed she wouldn't live up to the test [of recovering].)

Still taking the time to dress in the colorful *Tehuana* outfits she had worn for so many years, Frida received friends and relatives in her studio or in the canopied bed, depending on her health. When unable to dress herself, she asked her sister to help. Cristina was more than happy to oblige, but she had to divide her time between her new grand daughter Mara—the daughter of Isolda—and the Blue House where Frida lay. Whatever rivalries had existed between them, however Diego had acted to choose one over the other, seemed a thing of the past. It was a pact between sisters that brought Cristina and Frida together. In addition, Isabel Campos and a number of female friends from the neighborhood of Coyoacán saw her from time to time, unless Diego was around. His presence deterred them from talking freely, and he sometimes brought his daughter or a model or María Félix with him when he showed up. That company interrupted the socializing of the women and they could not feel at ease with him around. His loud voice and visitors took over the room and sidelined the women that Frida knew. There was no mixing.

Toward her final years, nurses stayed with her day and night. It appears that friends and relatives were careful to have someone by her side all the time, taking turns to keep Frida from lapsing into depression. Her bouts of melancholic silence became more frequent, and there are stories of several suicide attempts. As she exhibited more of the sadness her father had shown when she was young, Frida withdrew from conversations. Yet women brought their families with them to see her, even if for a few minutes. They were aware of her depressed states, her morphine, and her need for company all at the same time. The young girls who accompanied their mothers—mostly old friends of Frida who had traveled or worked with her over the years—found her "una señora linda, que olía rico, llena de vellitos como un durazno" (a pretty lady who smelled really nice, covered with soft hair like a peach) (Zamora 1987, 65–66). While she still received visitors, Frida was as she had always been: a combination of opposites.

On the one hand, she was the kind, frail, housebound woman in ribbons and rings who let little girls play with the combs and brushes in her purse and the dolls and knickknacks around the house; on the other, she fascinated them with her dirty language. Frida laughed with them as she used the bad words they had been taught to avoid. On good days, she could be counted on to entertain them with her exotic dresses and jewelry, and her house pets.

On the political front, Frida still had the will to be part of written protests in favor of universal peace and to defend Latin American sovereignty from foreign intervention, but she rarely went out of the house to participate in person. She spent hours typing letters that she and Diego would sign, and speeches for Rivera to give at Mexican Communist Party rallies. Before Frida was confined to bed permanently, she did find time to attend music concerts at *Bellas Artes*, film premieres in the cinema houses of Mexico City's historic center, and popular dance clubs such as the *Salón México*. Well-known culture critic Carlos Monsiváis recounts attending one of these concerts and the dramatic hush that fell over the audience as Frida entered the hall. Her appearance—and by then her myth—was as fascinating to the Mexican public as it had been to the society crowd of Paris and New York decades before. No one else had the long swishing skirts and dangling earrings she wore; and her perfume, a legacy of her Paris *Vogue* interview, wafted over the audience as well. She made an entrance even as she declared that she felt less attractive and less gifted than other women. Carlos Fuentes shares a similar experience. He recalls that before even laying eyes on Frida at a concert in *Bellas Artes*, he heard the jangling of her jewelry and the commotion accompanying her entourage. He likens her to "an Aztec goddess, perhaps Coatlicue, the mother deity wrapped in her skirt of serpents" (2005, 7) or a generic Earth Mother whose core was wounded but whose surface seemed intact.

Frida's insecurity extended to an implied and long-standing competition with her sister Cristina, seeing her as a rival and a natural beauty. Frida's overcompensation for her faults was the basis of her creation of a persona—the "Frida" that audiences have come to associate the real woman with. As her health waned, she could not continue that social activity, but she also avowed to close friends that she had grown tired of being relegated to second-class status by the Party. The role of women as secretaries and typists for the men was a big point of contention, and long before Frida was unable to dance or go out to other events, she had abandoned Party meetings. The ambivalent relationship she had had with the group continued throughout her lifetime. Diego's continued attraction to it (even as he was repudiated for his actions decades before), was at odds with her own feelings toward the organization's policies.

Like the allure of art, Frida's affirmed socialism, it seemed, was personal and not part of a formal institution. She lived art and politics in purely personal ways. As Carlos Fuentes writes in his introduction to the bilingual Spanish-English edition of her diary, "Frida... saw politics through Rivera. And Rivera was an anarchist, a mythomaniac, a compulsive liar, and a fantastic storyteller" (2005, 19). How those traits might be combined could either bode poorly for a political stance, since personal mythmaking contradicts the abolition of authoritarian figures underlying anarchism, or bode well for a charismatic figure who could twist politics to his will by weaving fabulous and fantastic tales around tenets that did not fit his own goals. That personal way of living in the world turned Frida into pretty good competition as a storyteller in her own right. Fuentes goes on to call her a "natural pantheist... involved in the glory of universal celebration... a priestess declaring everything created as sacred" (21). A strong case might be made in support of this statement if one points to the combination of her youthful energy, her art of vivid flora and fauna, her collection of dear pets, her fixation on human anatomy, her dreams of a child, a primitive (or Surrealist) fascination with the magical powers represented as inherent in the American continent, and her celebration of life even in adversity. In this vision, Frida as artist is also Frida as a creator of an animated universe, and at the same time one of its creations.

On the home front, writing in her diary became a solace for Frida, a way to work out her pain as painting had been in the years after the accident. Like her own body full of scars and wounds, and like the canvas surfaces of her paintings, the pages became a blank space on which to display her most intimate feelings. In the mid-1940s, after she had reunited with Diego and produced so many of her most famous and startling paintings, she began to write. Perhaps the sacrifices implied by the reunion stimulated her need to record things, to have an outlet for what she kept repressed. At first planned as a mere biographical record of dates and events, entries in this book became a regular part of her activities and a space for secrets, confessions, and verbal self-portraits parallel to her painted ones. The book itself had its own myth as an object of particular romanticism and esteem. Whether myth or reality, the initials J.K. on the leather binding were said to stand for John Keats, the person for whom the volume was originally intended. One of Frida's artist friends returned from a trip to New York with this gift, and Frida filled it with sketches and paragraphs, notes and observations, frustrations and dreams until the last days of her life. These pages contain an intimate portrait of a woman who wrote for herself, not for public scrutiny like her artwork. And there was no financial aspect to the diary as there was to the art; until she died, no one thought to delve into the depths of her written confessions for confidential information or for economic compensation. (Afterward, however, the volume became an object of contention; some were concerned about its contents and others were rumored to have removed incriminating pages.) In some ways, the paintings and the diary are mirror images of one another: the first a face for others to contemplate, and the second a private face for when emotions got the better of her. Diego was busy with his projects, and even though they left affectionate notes for one another, the diary became Frida's most constant companion and a source of brief emotional relief. The diary would not abandon her, nor would it talk back. It was always at her side. On its pages she could pour out her heart and even accuse those she no longer wished to confront in person.

The first pages of the diary hold line after line of word play and poetic images: from the sun and the moon to shades of red and green, from puns on the word elm and the proper name Olmedo (elm tree), to plays on links between the words martyr and material, from odes to Diego as her true son to letters to a departed love now lost in the mists of time. She wrote to her "dear diary" as so many women have done through the centuries, and her use of the familiar *tú* or "you" could mean that she is addressing either the book or Diego as much as an alter ego or an absent listener she yearned to have back at her side in troubled times. There are blue and brown and maroon drawings of human profiles, black birds, twirling vines, radiant suns, and lounging dogs. There is an entire page covered in the singular lines of thick blue ink she used that weave together tree branches, scrolls, leaves and flowers, and eyes. Amid the nine weeping eyes in the forest of foliage there is a full pair of lips not unlike her own, and a tiny shriveled object that looks like a worm, a piece of half-nibbled fruit, or even an early fetus. Above this are eight lines of prose that end in "y mi cuerpo se siente rodeado por tus brazos" (and my body feels enclosed and surrounded by your arms). As melancholy tinges the words relating the absence of a love, the gray-blue tint of this page creates a dark atmosphere of sadness. The arms as branches may have reached out to enfold her, but the emotion of those staring eyes is dark and longing: they are two separate beings disunited. Frida may have felt herself part of the forests and trees, linked underground by sinuous serpentine strands, but her human world looked torn apart, fragmented, and lonely. All of these words show up in the prose portions of the diary's pages, and they are echoed in the visual images.

Even when the pages are covered with big swirls of yellow and ochre paint, or bright geometric packaging (a chocolate wrapper reproduced), jagged teeth, broken body parts, and dark pools abound, continually lurking in the shadows. Lively colors seem to hide her more negative feelings and even the bright tones are set down in patterns of obsessive circles or forceful diagonal lines and striations. These are not peaceful rainbows but violent and contrasting pigments. A curious few pages show Frida as an Egyptian (one she labels Neferisis, another "Retrato de Neferúnico, Fundador de Lokura" (A Portrait of The One and Only Nefer, Founder of Craziness)). Reminiscent of her painted self-portraits on canvas, but now distorted, agitated, and apparently restless, the Middle-Eastern version of Frida in this portion of the diary has a third eye, although it is not formed by Diego this time. An exotic fez sits on her head, and a thick beard covers her face. Her gaze is toward the observer, but she does not look out to challenge us to an encounter but to stare blankly. She is Frida, but an estranged Frida made less Mexican and less approachable than ever before. Maybe as she felt less solid and less herself, she found such images could reproduce the emotional distance between inner and outer worlds, or maybe they reflect her readings. Maybe they are pure objects of her imagination.

This self-portrait is followed by pages of drawings of bullfighting scenes, popular dances, Aztec rituals complete with flames and steep pyramids, and multiple circles containing repeated variations on the faces of Frida and Diego. Their details are recognizable—his bulging eyes and thick lips, her pursed mouth and winged eyebrows—but they are reduced to caricatures. The climax of these images is a series of pages called "yo soy la desintegración" (I am disintegration personified). Feet, heads, arms, and legs protrude from swirling backgrounds to float disjointedly in mid-air. There are no whole bodies. Frida draws herself in pieces, her torso impaled on a marble column. Her earlier self-portrait that revealed a broken spinal column and a gaping wound in her back was more clinical; now the parts fly out in all directions with no chance for healing or cohesion. The haunting faces of overlapping circles are opposite to a page covered in prose, containing a stream-of-consciousness assortment of words: isolation, your hands, my eyes, magical ocean, Manhattan, I dream, light, music, gold, I dream, song, one line, one single line now. They culminate in a faded pencil outline of Yin and Yang, followed by the name "Stalin" and the date 1953. From this point on, references to politics ebb and flow from the diary entries amid Aztec sun symbols and classical-looking monuments. In 1954, the year she died, Frida did two paintings of Stalin—one called *Frida and Stalin* in which she is seen seated in a white *Tehuana* dress and red shawl in front of his portrait which she has painted, and the second, an unfinished portrait of a much younger Stalin. A third small

Masonite painting entitled *El marxismo dará salud a los enfermos* (Marxism will give health to the sick) encompasses a larger view of her private vision of politics, with a corseted Frida standing with a red book (of Mao?) in her left hand and being held up by a pair of embracing hands that reach out to steady her. Behind the hands are various symbols of different beliefs and ideologies: Karl Marx, a white dove, a terrestrial globe, a tiny Yin and Yang, a third eye. As the universe enfolds her, the painted Frida throws away her crutches. Not one element, but the unity of everything gives her life.

At least half a dozen pages of her diary contain the name DIEGO in tall, bold letters as if part of a scream. But this personal invocation of her *niño* (baby), as she constantly called him—both here and in person—is accompanied on facing pages by references to Stalin's death as the greatest loss of balance in world politics (with a bold "Viva Stalin, Viva Diego" right beside); a list of her heroes that runs from Engels and Marx to Lenin, Stalin, and Mao; a *calaca* or skeleton dressed in her own clothing; blood-red horses and grassy plains in flames; the practice drawing for a still life of fruit and vegetables; her pet dog Señor Xólotl dressed as an ambassador to a mythical Mayan empire; a self-portrait entitled *Alas rotas* (Broken wings); a headless Frida with only one leg; and a detached foot with painted toenails spanning two pages. If her diary is a hodgepodge of therapeutic confessions, poetic episodes, and primal fears all rolled into one, then the listed elements are a good example of the psychological exercise that she performed each time she opened a new page.

By August of 1953, Frida wrote of her deep concern about the amputation of her leg—a piece of medical advice seconded by her old friend Dr. Juan Farrill but a prospect that evoked terror in her—although she commented that it "will be a liberation" because she hoped to be able to walk alongside Diego once again. At least that is what she recorded before the fateful day, in the eternal hope of getting better. On April 27, 1954, Frida wrote of the operation: "salí sana" (I came out of it healthy) and proceeded to thank all the doctors, nurses, friends, and even the people of the Soviet Union and Mexico for their contributions to her healing. Her all-encompassing gratitude could have been an honest joy at having survived the procedure; but it also could reflect how much her "pantheism" extended into any and every living being. She was appreciative of any force that allowed her to keep going, and her surprise that she could forge ahead once again became mixed with wonder and gratitude, reflected here in a free association of names and people.

Between the month of April and July 13, 1954, when she died, Frida made a few last entries in the diary. There are not very many. A couple of them show her body with a dotted line across the amputated leg, others show her torso and limbs pierced by arrows just like the hunted deer she had painted years earlier. This time around, the deer is gone and she stands before herself (as the reader of the diary does) naked and alone. The last few entries in the volume contain what look like imagined geographies in primary colors alongside winged creatures, and her own face with the label "ENVIDIOSA" (the jealous woman). Of the last seven pages, one shows a running horse, one a copious series of teardrops, and five show human faces. In one sketch, a round-faced young Frida with dark, flat hair looks over the shoulder of another woman who is wearing a uniform with a starched white collar. This is one of her nurses, perhaps, and she saw herself as a little girl peering over to see what the adult was doing. Or maybe she was merely recording her feeling of powerlessness—as if becoming a child once again—in the face of the forces of the medical establishment. A return to childhood in this image is analogous to the unfinished painting of her family tree that was left on her easel in the Blue House. She may have lost her immediate connection to the world of the present, while the distant past of her family's roots and her own youth returned to inspire her. She could feel reunited with a younger self or with the branches of all her relatives through their images on canvas or paper.

Of the remaining entries, one includes her scrawled message of thanks to all of the forces that have helped her out once again, those that finally allowed her to leave the hospital. This time, she included her own "fuerza de voluntad" or sheer willpower as one of the sources of her release from those enclosed walls. The very last words she wrote refer to being discharged from the hospital after so many months of misery, but other messages have been read into them as well since they close the book on her life. Frida pens: "Espero alegre la salida—y espero no volver jamás" (I await my exit happily and I hope never to return). This is followed by one final bold lettered signature FRIDA. Some have read into the message that she was indeed content to leave the hospital, but that she felt her own end was near as well and looked to something beyond the pain she had long endured. One journey—from the medical facility back to her home—ran alongside another—the journey of life that ended in death. The "exit" conveys a dual sense of leaving something behind, but without remorse.

Frida's diary is another piece of evidence of the persistence of her creative spirit even as she suffered a great deal physically. From the operation in New York that some of her friends saw as the first step of a precipitous fall, Frida began her "exit." Even Rivera's fame couldn't completely cover her enormous medical expenses because, as Frida put it, "the [Mexican] *peso* isn't worth anything." The artist Arcady Boytler had added his financial support and, in appreciation of this, Frida had painted a few last self-portraits for him, such as the wounded deer in the forest. This was a gift to Boytler for his generosity. But, little by little, even her will to paint faded after 1950. Rivera would hire an indigenous man dressed in native gear to pose for him, and then he would send the man to Frida so that she could execute a portrait. There is one photo of Frida lying in a hospital bed, palette and brushes in hand, with the man standing next to her, smiling as she works. On the sheets lies a small canvas with some beginning brushstrokes, but no more. These are works she began, perhaps at Diego's insistence or maybe just to feel she had not lost her ability to paint, but they were never completed. She ran out of both time and energy.

She covered her fears with a mask of laughter, and many who knew her commented on Frida's delight in singing couplets and popular rhymes, or whistling them to a captive audience in her Blue House gardens. In the 1950s, these pastimes too faded away and her portraits always show the tears behind a mask of perseverance. In the last photographs taken of Frida—two or three of her in bed with a corset decorated as a testimony to the artist in her, and one as part of a political protest rally—she has only agony in her eyes. The morphine prescribed to her after the operations gave her a sense of calm that she found with nothing else, and it is conceivable that she had heavy doses before she left the hospital or received guests. She became addicted to that opiate, and during her last four years she kept a syringe of that narcotic or similar ones nearby at all times. Her physical and psychological dependence on these drugs grew until she could no longer function without them. Some have concluded that the side effects might have contributed to her death, given the weakened state of her organs. The female friends who saw Frida in her declining years commented on even finding syringes hidden in potted plants around the house.

In 1950 and 1951, Frida lay in excruciating pain, attended by medical personnel, servants in the house, and close friends such as Elena Vázquez Gómez, Teresa Proenza, Josefina Vicens, and Carlos Pellicer. Her older sister Matilde, who died only months after Frida did, wrote to the doctors to report the ill effects of her treatments such as infections and fevers that were the result of the sealed corsets and closed bandages. Those who visited noticed the smell around her coming from open wounds, and it became increasingly obvious that there would be no final cure despite Frida's desperate hope for one.

Diego was no longer a regular around Frida until shortly before her death. He came and went from her home but others were more constant.

He suffered from physical ailments of his own, and was always being treated for kidney problems or eye infections; he would die of heart failure in 1957, although he was diagnosed with cancer a year after Frida's death and went to the Soviet Union in search of a cure, or at the very least a treatment that would allow him to live a bit longer. As Frida lay ill, his social life continued unabated. Their friend, art critic Emma Hurtado, became his agent in 1946, and this is the woman he would marry in 1955, shortly after Frida died. In 1949, just before Frida underwent the most traumatic operations, he painted a portrait of the Mexican actress María Félix—the woman some called his one true love rather than Frida—in a gossamer lace gown that showed all her curves through its transparency. Newspaper and magazine interviews of Diego at the time revealed his denials, calling such rumors the vicious words of jealous women. Nevertheless, the portrait caused a lot of talk that got back to Frida. María Félix's name was included on the list that went around the walls of Frida's bedroom, names of women she called her true friends and those who had been frequent visitors at the Blue House. Yet Diego's ongoing infatuation with the actress went so far as to make Frida think once again of divorce. Given her state of health, this never went any further. María Félix was then in her heyday, an icon of the golden age of Mexican cinema and a larger-than-life star. Her beauty and defiant attitude—much more attributed to men than women in those days—sent Rivera to his knees. A dark-haired beauty on the silver screen would have been much more attractive to him than an addicted Frida who was losing touch with the real world. When Diego would go to her bedroom in the Blue House, he would find her in pain and rock her to sleep. Her desire to treat him as a child is thus reversed, and this shows a lasting tenderness between them. This was far from what he looked for in his flamboyant life, however, and María Félix came closer to his ideal. Frida and Diego remained married to the end, with only death separating them definitively despite all of the intervening reasons that might have caused their split.

How much the accident of 1925 contributed to her final demise is a point of debate, but so many cumulative problems existed that it would be hard to point to only one. After suffering through polio as a child, she had also been diagnosed with osteomyelitis and a variety of skeletal deformities including scoliosis. Add to this the problems with her internal organs that made her miscarry, and it is clear that she was headed for disaster. In the end, it was the perfect storm of diseases that attacked a weakened and decimated body no longer able to fight off infection. Frida's afflictions led to her addictions; between fears, a certain degree of hypochondria, psychological dependence, and physical maladies, she had no resistance left. Frida spent her last months outside the hospital in her room, carefully dressed and adorned by Cristina every morning, looking out the window into the garden. When her friends entered the room, sometimes she did not even turn around to face them. She no longer painted or wrote, and if she went out, she was confined to a wheelchair.

Photographs of Frida passively watching Diego work on murals for the top floor of *Bellas Artes* or chatting with visiting star Josephine Baker (both from 1952) show her seated, with people bending down to speak with her. Frida is recognizable by her long hair in a topknot, and by her colorful printed clothing. But her face is extremely thin and gaunt, her eyes sunken and dark in a chalk-white face. The rosy glow of her self-portraits has disappeared, and the opiates may have added to her pallor. Seen in profile, Frida smiles at Baker, a rising star of the dancehalls of Europe, but the animated gestures of the dancer and her entourage contrast with Frida's underplayed emotions. Aside from the phantom pain she often complained of from her amputated limb, Frida was no longer equal in height to others as she sat in the wheelchair, and therefore, for her, she was no longer an equal. The encounter with the celebrity looks more strained than joyous. In 1950, when Frida was confined to her hospital bed 24 hours a day to combat an infection caused by her lying prone for so long enclosed in the plaster corset, there is a photo of Diego leaning over her to kiss her. He is uncharacteristically dressed in a dark suit jacket and collared shirt. His face is not visible, but he seems to be kneeling to reach her lips. He is putting all his weight on his arms, and gently reaching across the bed. Frida has been decorated in her finest: a huge hair ribbon, three bracelets on one arm, a ring on each of the fingers of her left hand, dark lacquered nails, dangling earrings and lipstick. The hammer and sickle she painted on her body cast is visible above the bed covers. This condenses her identity and their relationship: Diego has gone to check on his "little girl" and he acts as if they were just greeting one another at the end of a regular workday. He kisses his bride as she cranes her neck to reach up to meet him. She has taken the care to dress up for him as if nothing were wrong. But the clash of feminine makeup and red political symbols captures her inner conflicts and paradoxes. The very last photograph taken of Frida and Diego together, a close up taken in 1954, reveals the ravages of age on his sagging face, and the scourge of disease on hers. Both are very pale. She clings to Diego's neck as if not wanting to let go, and they don't look each other in the eye but gaze off into space. During her last, painful years, Frida and Diego did a sort of social dance around one another, but each knew the end was fast approaching.

Sensing that time was not on Frida's side, Diego hastily tried to arrange a show of her work at the *Instituto Nacional de Bellas Artes*, but Frida would not live to see his plan come to fruition. It took a lot to coordinate such a large project and neither of them was in the shape to go it alone. While there would not be the exhibit Diego wished for her, however, on April 13, 1953, she would attend another opening, when Frida was finally celebrated in an homage to her life's work: a one-woman show. The *Galería de Arte Contemporáneo*, right in the middle of the most vibrant part of downtown Mexico City, and owned by famous photographer Dolores Alvarez Bravo (wife of even more famous Mexican photographer Manuel Alvarez Bravo), was the space chosen for this exhibit. Frida was ecstatic. She painted the original invitation herself, and gathered paintings from friends' collections to complete the display. Frida was in terrible health by then, and no one knew if she would make an appearance at the opening. It had even been arranged to take her four-poster canopied bed to the gallery to reproduce as faithfully as possible the atmosphere in which she had worked on the paintings while lying in it. At the last minute, an ambulance arrived with Frida lying on a stretcher. Surrounded by her friends, she was taken into the building and put into the bed as if she were at home. The Mexican painter Dr. Atl, and a host of other supporters, admirers, and art collectors, accompanied her for several hours. It came late in life, but Frida was present at her show whether she walked there on her own or not. Reporters interviewed her, and she reiterated the fact that she was not sick but "broken" and, as she put it, still able to paint so still alive. After Breton's invitation to be part of the Paris exhibition so many years before, this was Frida's second big chance to put her art on display, attended with such excitement and enthusiasm from the press.

On July 2, 1954, Diego wheeled Frida out to participate in a protest march against American intervention in Guatemala's presidential elections; she looked pale even as she held her fist up in protest. She would not be seen in public again. Family and friends went to commemorate her birthday on July 7, but they had to wait for the effects of the morphine to wear off before they could have the festivities. Six days later, Frida died. One account said she died in her sleep, another that she went into the bathroom and died there. Early that morning, when he received the news of her death, Diego went to contemplate her one last time, quiet and in peace. The doctor's regular visit to check on her, arranged each evening for the next morning, went ahead as scheduled, since he couldn't be reached in time to cancel.

Coming only one week after her forty-seventh birthday, Frida Kahlo's death on July 13, 1954, came as no surprise to her friends or to Mexicans in general, who had become used to associating her with suffering. She had been ill most of her adult life, and modern medical science had little more to offer her than some small amount of relief from her pain. Faith in science led her to seek treatments, but she suffered from pains that were emotional as well as physical. Diego Rivera, the man she had chosen to marry despite warnings from parents and relatives, had been difficult from the beginning. His relationships with so many women could not have helped her mental state as she tried to cope with operations and treatments. A second round of marriage had not resolved any issues. The recent amputations of her right foot and then more of her leg were obvious signs of how serious things were; there was to be no getting better. That last public appearance at the political rally against U.S. involvement in Guatemala and in support of that country's recently-elected president Jacobo Arbenz showed just how far her health had deteriorated. If Frida had been spending most of her time out of the public eye, now all could see how she had changed for the worse. Politics brought her out into the street, but chronic illness made activity difficult. She did not rise from her wheelchair, which was pushed in turns by her husband, Diego Rivera, and by other artist friends such as Juan O'Gorman. While she chanted slogans and held a placard mounted on a long stick, Frida barely moved. Even sitting still, she was in agony. Wrapped in a flowing white scarf and uncharacteristically dark clothing, with a constant expression of excruciating pain on her face, Frida looked as pale as a pen-and-ink etching on parchment. After her release from the hospital in 1951, her close friends had slept on cots in her bedroom to be near her and, more often than not, to administer the injections of drugs that kept the pain at bay. But now the end was clearly at hand; she lasted but a few days longer.

But in death, as in life, Frida was also more than what met the eye. For four decades, she had been the constant center of personal contradictions and passionate politics, and so it was at the end as well. Her body had always been the subject of her art, and in the end it was her body's breakdown that was witnessed by all. As her life's energy flowed away, she once again took to the streets in support of a political cause even in her last days. At her side was Diego Rivera, the painter chosen by presidents to create murals on the walls of public buildings in honor of Mexico's heroic past and the impetus for her activities. He was also, since their first fateful meeting, both the inspiration for art and a source of pain in Frida's life. Upon her death days later, he insisted that her body lie in state in the rotunda of the beautiful art deco *Museo del Palacio de Bellas Artes* (Museum of the Fine Arts Palace) in the center of downtown Mexico City, where he had wanted her exhibition to be held. This was, after all, where his art had been displayed for all to see, and where people of national importance were given a final public farewell. Old flame and longtime friend—some say her only true love—Alejandro Gómez Arias brought the Communist flag to be draped over her coffin, at Diego's insistence. The act was more symbolic than anything, since Frida's opinion of the Party had been made clear long before. Diego had recently petitioned to be reinstated into its ranks, and this was more a statement of his allegiance than it was of Frida's. He was delighted when his petition was accepted. Whether the placement of the flag was an act to call attention to himself, or a genuine salute to her politics, it certainly created a stir. Like so much in Frida Kahlo's life, it is hard to untangle the personal and the political, and even harder to come up with a single story. The yellow hammer and sickle on a red background certainly provoked many reactions to the association of this well-known artist with faith in a particular doctrine and party. That she had been at the center of political storms, however, was indeed true.

At the funeral ceremony, ex-president Lázaro Cárdenas took his place at the center of events. Having been out of office for over a decade, replaced by Manuel Avila Camacho (who did not attend the funeral), in making an appearance Cárdenas perpetuated the link between intellectuals and the policies of his government. Under Cárdenas, Trotsky had been given entry into Mexico and Diego had been chosen as one of the painters of the Revolution. At Frida's final farewell, politicians and artists mingled around her flag-draped coffin and cascades of flowers fell on all sides. Diego looked haggard and drawn, dressed in an oversized gabardine overcoat with huge dark circles under his eyes. His baggy clothing and unkempt hair made his own death—a mere three years later—seem even closer. Despite their tempestuous relationship over the years, he looked like he had just lost his best friend. On again, off again, Frida and Diego had always kept in touch and had even lived side-by-side in connecting studios for a while despite their divorce and subsequent remarriage. Diego's daughter Guadalupe Rivera was there too, and Frida's sister Adriana Kahlo de Veraza. For some, it was a personal tragedy; for others, it was a public statement.

Never as much the faithful party comrade as a spirited young woman intoxicated with sexuality, politics, and youth, Frida thus became a political symbol at her own funeral. Not everyone in attendance agreed that her role was to represent an organized group, and each had his or her memories of her. Many, such as Gómez Arias, knew her as part of that collection of lively and rebellious characters, the *Cachuchas*. Her classmates, the students she had taught later on, and the many international friends she had cultivated over the years had all shared different experiences with her. In her short life, Frida Kahlo had been in the public eye of a country of which she was so proud to be a part. Like the date she chose as her birth year—three years after the real one—1910 was the beginning of a modern

Mexico and the beginning of a modern woman's life. The successes and failures of post-Revolutionary Mexico ran parallel to the triumphs and tragedies of Frida Kahlo. Each had to deal with questions of identity; each had to figure out how to sort out the legacies of the past without sacrificing the future; each had to survive challenges that threatened their existence. At home, Frida said she always felt like part of a great family; when she was away, she couldn't wait to return. Like Mexico, she was so much more than the sum of individual (and sometimes contradictory) parts.

A great number of people went to see Frida one last time, from dignitaries to neighbors from Coyoacán. In a light drizzle, her body was transported to the nearby *Panteón de Dolores* (Cemetery of Grief) where she was cremated. Poets and classmates praised how she had remained the same young Frida at heart despite the difficulties she had confronted. As the flames consumed her body, Diego, friends, and *Los Fridos* sang the *Internacional* and a collection of Mexican popular songs from the times of the Revolution. The mix was a fitting tribute to all the different aspects of her life. Then Diego took her ashes in a pre-Columbian urn and placed them on her bed in the Blue House. But when the house opened as a museum, the urn scared visitors, so it was removed. A commission was set up by Diego to ensure that all of their possessions would be turned over to the Mexican people. This has been honored. Nearing the end of his own life, Diego declared that he wanted his own cremated ashes to be mixed with Frida's so they would be indistinguishable, but the Mexican government had other ideas. Rivera's family accepted the offer of space in the same cemetery where Frida was cremated, but in the specially designated *Rotonda de los Hombre Ilustres* (Hemicycle of Illustrious Men). He was not cremated, and he rests under a monument built in his honor. Even in the same city, they are so near and yet so far from one another.

A few months after Frida died, Diego's daughter Ruth Rivera took her family to live in the Blue House. There, her daughter was baptized with Diego and María Félix present as godparents. The house was opened to the public in 1958, and includes some of Frida's last paintings, showing her family and a still life. Her bedroom as she was used to keeping it, her folksy kitchen where she prepared meals for Diego, some of her many *Tehuana* dresses and rings, colorful papier-maché masks, Judas figures that were traditionally filled with fireworks and set off the Saturday before Easter, and paintings by friends Marcel Duchamp, Yves Tanguy, and Paul Klee are displayed. The ceramic dishes given to Frida as a newlywed are here, as well as a tiny fraction of Diego's pre-Hispanic art collection. Called a museum, the Blue House looks more like a home where residents Frida, Guillermo, Matilde, Cristina, Diego, or Trotsky might emerge at any time into the central patio to enjoy the sun.

Chapter 6

THE LEGACIES OF "FRIDA"

The line winds from the fancy ironwork doorway of the *Palacio de Bellas Artes* in Mexico City, through the small park outside, all the way to the edge of Juárez Avenue that runs in front of the art deco building. Organ grinders, sweet-sellers, and other entrepreneurs offer what they have to sell patient visitors or ask for a donation. Visitors from Italy, Germany, the United States, France, Belgium, Argentina, other parts of Mexico, and elsewhere around the globe wait for their turn to enter the white marble building with the copper dome. Banners flap in the breeze, announcing the event all are there for: Frida Kahlo 1907–2007. The world is celebrating Frida's centennial and Mexico has gone all out to call attention to her.

Between June 13 and August 19, 2007, 69 individual collectors, public institutions, government agencies, and private foundations collaborated to put together a comprehensive retrospective view of the life and work of this important artist and Mexican citizen. After 100 years, Frida has become a true Mexican cultural icon as a woman of passion, will, survival, and talent. All of these qualities were celebrated in this exhibition, which was accompanied by round tables, discussion groups, keynote lectures, and a special edition catalogue to commemorate the event. There were also coordinated events at bookstores and art galleries around Mexico City, across the United States, and in Europe. In Havana, an exhibit entitled *Desde la piel de Eva y con los ojos de Adán* (from Eve's skin and with Adam's eyes) opened simultaneously with the Mexico City event. The year 2007 was definitely the year of Frida Kahlo. Even a competition of popular singers held in Havana, Cuba, sponsored by the Mexican Embassy there honored Frida's politics and social stance. This was touted as a celebration of her upholding the social and cultural values shared by the Cuban and Mexican nations, values now embodied in her art. The winner went to Mexico to join the festivities in *Bellas Artes*. It was a celebration not to be missed.

Consisting of over 354 pieces—65 oil paintings, several lithographic prints, a good number of unedited documents, manuscripts, 50 private letters, personal memoirs of friends, and about one hundred photos from her own collection—the homage to Frida covered just about every aspect of her life, from the political to the artistic and from her earliest years to her last. Since these items had not previously been accessible to the Mexican public, people traveled from all over the capital as well as from every part of the nation to gain the most detailed view of Frida's life for the first time. The heavy investment in upgrading the display areas of *Bellas Artes* to accommodate the works of art and photographs on all four floors of the building, to install new facilities to keep the temperature and humidity at perfect levels, and to maintain the obviously increased presence of security was certainly worth it. The turnout was enormous, the reaction enthusiastic.

On the top floor of the building, spectators could begin with early photographs of Frida's parents and grandparents, her sisters and herself at a very young age. The closeness between father and daughter is evident in the number of photos she kept from their travels on the streets of Mexico City to record the government's modernizing campaign and the preservation of traditional structures. The influence of Guillermo on Frida's vision of Mexican society, her strategy of moving in for the close-up rather than the bird's eye view—just as her father had done with the Post Office building, new suburban houses, or old haciendas that were being divided up for new homes—evolves from the camera's eye that she was already used to before she began to paint. In addition, later canvases of her family lineage or herself as a hybrid woman uniting strands of European and Mexican descent were fed directly from the pictures that recorded her family's bloodlines. Frida would not, of course, become a photographer but she would use her self-portraits as documents of her emerging identity. Although painters and photographers were pitted against one another as two types of (competing) artists in the early years of George Eastman's promotion of the camera, by the time Guillermo and Frida inherited these traditions, they saw them as linking and not separating their work.

Although Mexico celebrated Frida's artwork in exhibits in 1974, 1983, and 2004 alongside similar events in the United States, Japan, Great Britain, and Spain, the year 2007 witnessed the most extensive and comprehensive display of everything related to the woman and the artist. Even the *Bellas Artes* salon named for Diego Rivera was taken over for Frida's portraits, still lifes, self-portraits, and urban landscapes. Tina Modotti, the Italian photographer who adopted Mexico as her home, appears alongside Frida at political meetings in the rooms dedicated to that aspect of her life. Historical documents, notes, and essays stand next to the art, letters, diary pages, photos, and other examples taken from her everyday life to place everything in context. One intriguing room holds her water colors and commentaries on the exquisite visual beauty of Japanese and Chinese calligraphy. Rounding out the show are two sketches belonging to Frida's niece Isolda Kahlo Pinedo that have never been displayed before. From the most public to the most intimate levels, Frida comes alive in this tribute that suggests the many ways she has influenced people and touched their lives.

At the significant distance of 100 years after her birth, a resurgence of interest in Frida as an artist and as a woman has begun, but not for the first time. Over the last 30 years especially, Frida has been in the eye of a global public in international museums, Mexican and Hollywood films, European and American fashion shows, and even television programs dedicated to her. In 2007, simultaneous exhibits in San Diego, Philadelphia, San Francisco, and at the Walker Arts Center in Minneapolis, Minnesota, celebrated her art and her life, with the biggest festival of all being held at the *Museo del Palacio de Bellas Artes* right in the middle of downtown Mexico City. With the entire museum dedicated to her canvases, photographs, popular arts and crafts, and a detailed historical timeline, the exhibit is just one piece of an even grander and more extensive mosaic. The phrase "Cultural tourism with Frida" is being promoted by tourist agencies and airlines as a way to get to know Mexico, and the lines outside the museums and galleries prove it is working. Frida has opened the doors to Mexico like few other national figures have managed to do.

The centennial exhibit was certainly unique and unequaled in its all-encompassing content. But at the same time, the unveiling of a treasure trove of lost documents and artwork by Frida and her husband Diego Rivera, hidden away behind a wall in Frida's Blue House for fifty years, added to the excitement and attraction for admirers from around the world. A pact of silence for half a century kept these objects from the public eye but years passed, and the collection became part of the *patrimonio nacional* or national patrimony belonging to all Mexicans, regardless of where they live. The works of many famous artists are on display in formal collections around the world, yet their lives remain hidden behind their paintings, of less interest to the average person. Yet Frida still seems so alive even five decades after her death, each generation adding meaning to her life and work. The historical woman Frida Kahlo and the artistic face of "Frida" still speak to crowds of visitors in the twenty-first century, no matter where they are from or how old they are. For all his fame and notoriety, Diego Rivera does not hold the charismatic power over an audience that Frida does. The fiftieth anniversary of his death in 2007 was indeed quietly commemorated, while Frida's centennial brought throngs to the streets. The celebrations of her centennial just reaffirm that there is a subterranean current of Kahlo-related interest throughout the world. One day before the Kahlo Centennial opened in Mexico City, it was announced that the documents of all types belonging to Frida and Diego that had been stashed and sealed away until fifty years had passed since Rivera's death were due to be opened. So that it would not overshadow the *Bellas Artes* event, this "intimate" archive would be released little by little as it was inventoried, digitalized, and officially recorded. While what was discovered under lock and key until both of them had been gone for decades would not change the public's perception of them that much, the items will certainly add details to any study of their life together, and multiply the faces of Frida that admirers recognize. An inventory of her closet reveals shawls, dresses, and even a tiny red boot that fit over the stump left after her foot was amputated.

The years of Frida's life filled in by her biographical data have a greater significance for more readers today than at other historical times. In the 1960s, for instance, when tourists from the United States flocked to the beaches of Acapulco and only a few of the pyramids had been unearthed at Teotihuacan, the Blue House and Anahuacalli had been open to the public for a couple of years but did not attract the throngs of today. Diego's more museum-like house was a place for exhibitions, not a home. Frida's home, recently refurbished and spectacularly blue with pink trim in the middle of that paradise called Coyoacán, had some visitors, but not as many as would visit decades later. Steady trickles of guests walked through the halls, rooms, and leafy patio, but Frida Kahlo was not yet a household name or a superstar. Not all of the diary pages and the artwork were on display, but the architecture she had inhabited was visible for the initiated. Coyoacán was still a distance from the cathedral and the *zócalo* or public square at the center of the city; it wasn't easy to get there and there wasn't always an impelling reason to make the trip. Besides, the artists most associated with Mexico were still Rivera, Siqueiros, and Orozco. Women were not yet on the cultural map.

Beginning in the 1980s, things changed dramatically. To start, an exhibit opened at the Whitechapel gallery in London in 1982; it was dedicated to two women whose paths had crossed in history and whose heroic lives were inspirational to waves of feminists in Europe: Tina Modotti and Frida Kahlo. Modotti's photographs and the face of Frida leaped out in all their glory to meet the gaze of visitors from near and far. The essays in the exhibition catalogue opened the eyes of artists, scholars, and culture critics; the commentaries of Laura Mulvey and Peter Wollen were especially welcomed in academic circles that were using feminist language to talk about the fields of art, literature, and culture. Feminist art criticism was on the rise along with the political movements that fostered it, and these critics established gender and art as exciting crossover categories of analysis. Not alone by any means, both Mulvey and Wollen, however, brought women and Mexican art into the forefront of consideration on other continents, and they turned the gaze of critics from the frescoes and murals of the so-called holy trinity—Siqueiros, Rivera, and Orozco—to the paintings of Kahlo and the photography of Modotti. In 1983, they made a film entitled *Frida Kahlo and Tina Modotti* that compares and contrasts the styles and subject matter of these two women working in the heady days of post-Revolutionary Mexico.

A champion of modern art since 1901, the Whitechapel Gallery where Frida made her first spectacular appearance has premiered international artists such as Pablo Picasso, Jackson Pollock, and Mark Rothko, and has been a showcase for British artists from Lucian Freud and Peter Doig to Mark Wallinger. With a track record that includes displaying Picasso's Spanish civil war protest painting *Guernica* in 1939, this gallery has contributed to the promotion of the newest and most innovative and has introduced the European public to artists of the Americas. What has been called the so-called Fridamania of the past thirty years probably had some of its earliest roots in the 1982 exhibit. Adding to the gallery exhibit, Hayden Herrera's groundbreaking biography of Frida Kahlo published in the mid-1980s, and Mexican art critic Raquel Tibol's studies of her art in the 1990s, expanded the attention paid to this icon of women's art.

Since then, museums, galleries, universities, and popular venues have returned many times to revisit "Frida" in her self-portraits and, in 2008, in her still lifes (Herrera and Grimberg 2008). In 1990, the Metropolitan Museum of Art in New York City had a vast exhibit called *Mexico: Splendors of Thirty Centuries*. The exhibition catalogue, with a prologue by Mexican philosopher Octavio Paz, addressed the context for the rise of artists such as Diego and Frida and made several references to both of their works. In a decade of increasing immigration from Mexico to the United States, paying attention to the history of that culture, as well as its most important artists, was a good choice. The show was a Met blockbuster. By the 1990s,

Frida had become an established component of the canonical history of Mexican art, her home was the destination of hundreds of travelers, and Hollywood stars were investing in her paintings when they came up at auction. Actresses such as Madonna and Salma Hayek vied to play Frida in various cinema productions, and Madonna spent a lot of money on a couple of Frida's paintings. She insisted on buying "My Birth," the shocking and bloody scene painted in 1932 that showed a woman covered in a sheet giving birth to what looks like a full-sized and stillborn Frida. The Madonna of Pain picture hanging on the wall behind the bed witnesses the atrocity that gives death instead of life. Tabloids reported that Madonna wanted to hang the picture—which she successfully won—in her bedroom. There was no doubt about it: Hollywood had found a new icon and Frida was here to stay. Everything related to Frida was full of symbolism and could be interpreted anew with each and every glance.

The twenty-first century has not changed the spotlight on Frida, her life story, her suffering, and her survival as a creative spirit rather than becoming a victim of all her difficulties. She is still the face of abused women, women abandoned by their partners, women who suffer serious health issues, women who try to break into the art world, women who feel themselves living between cultures and nations, and Chicana women who use her face morphed onto the outline of the celestial blue garment of the Virgin of Guadalupe as a guiding figure for their social and political identities. She is conflict personified, the fragile made strong, carnality and spirituality rolled into one. The episodes of her life painted or sketched or written into her diary kept the disintegration of her body—which she feared was always around the corner or lurking in the shadows—at bay. Like Sheherezade of the *Thousand and One Nights* tales whose stories staved off death, Frida painted to keep the *calaca*—Mexico's female figure of death that is conjured up at popular festivals, mocked in costume and mask, but is still a source of great anxiety—at arm's length. When she got too close for comfort, the colors or the scenes displayed that terror.

Today, the face of Frida can be found even when least expected. From invitations to attend a Frida Kahlo Knitting Circle, to all sorts of decorations for the home available on the Internet for immediate delivery, some offered alongside an E-Bay auction of the steel pick used by Ramón Mercader to kill Trotsky right in Frida's Blue House backyard; from extravagant and colorful Frida costumes complete with eyebrowed mask for Halloween festivities, to a lavish spread of architectural photographs in the June 2005 issue of the British magazine *The World of Interiors*, dedicated to beautiful homes of beautiful stars such as Kahlo; to *Florida International Magazine's* annual art issue of October 2005 with a model decked out in maroon velvet and covered in turquoise jewelry with Frida's makeup, hairstyle, earrings, and ribbons, staring at us boldly, there is little doubt that Frida Kahlo is still with us, if not in exactly the same guise as two decades ago. Even though the *Florida International* spread is titled "Channeling Frida Kahlo," companion pieces in the issue deal with art, passion, and aphrodisiacs. These seem to draw lines straight to Frida as passionate woman, creative spirit, and lover. There is always something new or different to connect her with. Among the last words in her diary, her last wish perhaps, Frida almost opens the door to a never-ending appropriation: "Espero alegre la salida y espero no volver jamás" (I happily await my exit, and I hope never to return). Her physical disappearance from the scene of history has not had any impact whatsoever on the ubiquitous recycling of her face as a type of shorthand for innumerable stories, and for the use of everyone who has suffered in their rewriting of her legend. In fact, it would be difficult to find an emptier vessel to fill than her torn body and tortured narrative. Frida is like the chalk outline of the victim that police detectives draw at the scene of the crime: her story is there to be filled in by each retelling.

But a relationship with the figure of "Frida" and to the objects revolving around her could hardly remain the same over time with the rise of the complex social relations that characterize global culture in the twenty-first century. It is true, of course, that the value of her original artworks has been preserved for the financially able, connecting purchasers today with Frida's painted world of yesterday through the medium of money that takes one right back to some lost moment in the past when she put her brush to Masonite board. The genuine article—one of her canvases or drawings—transports the observer back to Frida's side to feel as she did. Yet Frida is also part of the mass market of those with fewer investment funds, a genuine heroine of popular culture, with reproductions holding special meaning for fans as much as they find in collected items related to movie stars and rockers. Her face is as familiar as the photos periodically rediscovered in the dusty family albums at the back of the closet. Since 1982, Frida has been like one of the family.

For many, Frida belongs like a family member on Day-of-the-Dead altars among other icons of personal loss, alongside the Virgin of Guadalupe, photos of deceased relatives and fading ancestors. A sign of the traumas of modern times, Frida's face can be company in grief. As her face collapses into masks, fragments, and Andy Warhol-like repetitions on stamps and matchbooks and t-shirts, the temptation arises to impose an ending on her story, even as she dissolves into ephemeral moments and fleeting encounters. The products are easier to acquire, though, than a happy ending to the story. But that may be the greatest attraction of all: there is no ending, just the invitation to add to the story. Frida is a mystery that will never be solved.

As commercial products, and even ideas, increasingly cross open geographical boundaries, Frida is an icon of familiarity and consolation that can be read as unchanging despite all of the other reorganizations of a globalized world. Dead for over 50 years now, "Frida"—not the historical woman Frida Kahlo, just plain Frida—lives on in a peculiarly static universe of eternal suffering. The tears of Mexican soap opera divas have found an audience more scattered across borders than many would have ever imagined, but Frida's tears remain visible as one of the last remnants of what looks like a genuine internal, private, emotion made public. She did not use glycerine as the stars do, however; her tears were mirrors of real pain. The repetition of the look on her face is a repeat performance because it resurfaces so many times but she does not lose that sense of genuine grief. "Frida" is the real deal.

In its repetition across her 1940s self-portraits, but especially in *The Mask* (1945), a blotchy conglomeration of reds and dark pigments that covers but also reveals, she has reached a point at which the tear is only an ornament on the woman's face. In fact, this painting recalls the Man Ray extreme close-up photograph of the 1930s entitled *Larme (Tear)*. Close enough to see her pores, but abstracted enough from the actual woman photographed to see only skin, eyes, and glycerine-like droplets almost frozen on her cheek, the spectator must focus on what is actually invisible: what was it that provoked the tear to accumulate, then fall from the eye? Now rendered emotionless, the woman holds the evidence of that something, but the effect is strangely cold. No longer even attached to a warm or real human face, but instead at the center of focus with the surface of the skin as backdrop, the tear is a mask in and of itself. Frida Kahlo was acquainted with Man Ray and his photographic work, but his frozen drop of water lies at the opposite pole from her own continual flow of mournful droplets until the last few years of her life. By 1945, a decade before her death, Frida Kahlo's *The Mask* shows a similar operation at work as Man Ray's model with glycerine tears. We have seen her tears so many times, in so many forms, that in the end they are an expected and intrinsic part of a portrait on which we can write a story of interpretation but behind which we will never really penetrate. And so tears become a weapon to safeguard what lies behind them.

An unemployed woman living in the Mexican states of Michoacán or Veracruz, for instance, might find companionship in Frida's tears as she mourns a lost friend or relative who has gone north to make a better living. If the news reaches home that the loved one has died, then Frida could signify the pain shared by Mexican women across centuries for different reasons. Like a new female Greek chorus of lamentation behind the politics playing out in the foreground of national dramas, including presidential elections, the violence of narco-traffickers, immigration debates and woes, and vigilante justice, women especially have raised Frida up as one of their own. In the shantytowns of Ciudad Juárez or Tijuana, just waiting to run across the border in a second, third or even fiftieth attempt to make it across to paradise, Frida's painted self-portrait on the border is evoked once again. She went with Diego on commissions, it is true, but she did not feel any less alien in her new surroundings than another immigrant to a country that is not home. Border agents and customs deputies do not reflect feelings; a woman casting her emotions onto colorful canvases does. The differences between Kahlo and Rivera in the realm of painting can be explained in part as gendered reactions to cultural events: for one, the world was a place of opportunity, for the other it brought new and unexpected anxieties and grief. Official government rhetoric made the Revolution a masculine enterprise, from historical events to artistic achievements, and Frida was no different from other women who felt on the margins of the national project. In the twenty-first century, Mexican men have gone abroad to work for better wages and send them back to the women and children who remain behind. The parallels are interesting.

Frida sat at the same cultural and geographic juncture of the border between the United States and Mexico that many do today, but the geography didn't look quite the same in 1932 as it does now. Entire cities have grown up on the industry of immigration, while in the early twentieth century the border was emptier. This doesn't mean to imply that cultural rather than geographical borders did not exist, however. Despite the early suggestion of confrontation she included in her juxtaposed images of the myths of Mexico and the United States in the painting *Frida on the Border*, Frida stands in the middle of these cultural divisions and discrepancies in a stance of sheer resistance and rose-colored glory. She erects a pedestal on which to place herself, dressed in an immaculate pink dress (*rosa mexicano* in all its bright visibility) and shoes to match, with opera-length gloves and cigarette in hand, astride a division between nature (Mexico) and culture (the United States). One might well imagine that there is an element of satire implicit in the construction of such a monument to herself as an individual when the nation, first under President Ortiz Rubio and then his successor Abelardo Rodríguez that same year, is in the process of codifying its values in public monuments and murals. Her own figure monumentalizes that process and comments on it at the same time. So her full-length self-portrait becomes a condensed version of a collective movement of commemoration.

Yet there is also a hint of the untouchable essence of the woman who defies both cultures: she does not topple from her perch; she is not torn in two (yet). She hears the siren's song coming from the north but it has been interpreted for her by a superstar: namely, Diego, who wants international fame. She might show tears because he speaks for her and creates the situation that places her in-between, far from the friends and family she knows. To set her fairly diminutive self on display calls attention to dreams and to absences, to technology and to forlorn women. She has not abdicated her role as witness as she does a year later in *My Dress Hangs There*, now fully engulfed by the geography of Manhattan but physically and emotionally absent. Her clothing remains behind as the only witness to her existing at all. Part of the archaeological ruins of the big city, the dress is a monument emptied of life. It is up to the spectator to fill in that dress, to imagine her on that island, just as one wonders why the tears are provoked. She has taken the first step toward becoming the chalk outline of crime stories. Like stones left on a path through the woods or tree branches bent as signals to lead back home when an adventure is finished, Frida left self-portraits to find her way home. She desperately wanted to be in Mexico; with Diego, all the better, but alone if that were the only way.

If we look at the black and white photograph reproduced by Emma Dexter and Tanya Barson in their wonderful essay in the 2005 Tate exhibition catalogue (22), we see Frida Kahlo, the real person, surveying a quiet street in Laredo, Texas, sheltered from the hot sun by a canopy and framed in the distance by two signs. Both are partially hidden, but by filling in the blanks as with her artwork, the word "BORDER" becomes legible and the other is a sign with the name "FIDEL." The double language tells us the geography: a mixture of two cultures and two isolations. A single figure dressed in white strolls along the other, shadier, side of the sidewalk and four men stand immediately behind Frida. Laredo appears predictably empty, almost dream-like, still a desert fantasy to be filled in and not a nightmare discovered too late to escape. Frida gazes out at sand and sky; few human forms enter her vision. Today, the same landscape represents other absences—those who have crossed the border and made it or those who have tried and been less successful. Kahlo's bright dress hanging empty in Wall Street is a remnant, like the plastic bags and empty water bottles left behind on the ground as desert phantoms cross the border into unknown and terrifying territory. The horror of the moment is left only in the archaeological traces, something so popular with the tourist trade in

Teotihuacan and other official sites. Like the footprints of immigrants, Frida's portraits mark the passing of other people and other cultures not so evident in formal statements made by governments.

NAFTA's free trade policies—carved out in the early 1990s among Canada, Mexico, and the United States—have had deep and lasting effects on more than one economy and culture. Part of the circulation of goods and products has been the iconizing of "Frida," who flows easily in and out of all the nations of the hemisphere. The face of this tiny woman seems so harmless, so reassuring, so nostalgic for a time when Mexico was a place to visit and not a contentious border. The Mexico of more than one Hollywood Western was a mysterious and exotic land where criminals fled to be safe from the law, where artifacts sold in market stalls and not on the internet, and where life may have been hard but it was sunny and colorful. The romantic image of the border in the equally romantic frame of a photograph encloses a past which, of course, also produced tears that no one saw until Frida Kahlo came along. Frida dared to focus on the otherwise faceless masses of the great Mexican popular classes painted by Rivera on the walls of the National Palace and the *Secretaría de Educación Pública* (National Secretary of Education); she opened the lives of Mexican women to public view. Like the soap operas set inside Mexican homes—rich and poor—her portraits let spectators into the private life of a person rather than show the sweeping epics of national history. This shift in viewpoint humanizes emotions and brings cultures together, clustered around the suffering image. The similarities between religious icons and the secular ones so popular in Mexican *retablos* or altars are made evident in the reverence of Frida's features as symbols for an entire people. There are abundant paradoxes both reflected and created by the many recognizable faces of Frida.

For some, Frida's portraits are allegories of today's society in the throes of crisis. Her personal situation reflects the embattled situations and experiences of people today. Unfaithful spouses, lost children, not-so-secret affairs: all would certainly bring a tear to the strongest personality. So the use of Frida's face on objects that can accompany those who suffer carries the weight of shared emotional burdens: her scars are ways to represent other, less visible wounds. This has been the case for some recent immigrants, lesbian communities, women in prison in Chile, and those with serious diseases. All of these are interesting paradoxes since, like Ché Guevara, Eva Perón, and Elvis Presley, stars of politics and performance she has been compared to, Frida is an enigma hard to decipher but filled with empathy by nature. All had causes, all suffered (two from illness and one from government retaliation), and all died leaving a larger-than-life legend.

Transient lives all four, dead in mid-life, maybe the fear and mystery of their very disappearance is the motivation for a desire to save their images. If the faces of Frida attest to a visible staying power long beyond their physical death, the ability to buy into them could foster the belief that the transience of life is contradicted and even possibly conquered. Whatever threats appear in life, there is always the reassurance of company in the beautiful face of a young, blonde Evita or the stoic face of Frida that never ages. The two men and two women evoke both melancholic loss and something to hang on to. With many of the west's traditional categories gone—no more divided Berlin, no more Soviet Union, no more trade barriers in North America—Frida now stands in for a collective loss of compass. Even if governments make decisions that have repercussions in the long run, in day-to-day life Frida is an identifiable woman that shares our pain. Can she, like Dorothy's magic shoes in *The Wizard of Oz*, be a vehicle back to simpler times and places, a reassurance that the Mexican workers on the border are part of a culture whose tragedies we all share or, conversely, that are as fragile behind their stoic faces as she is? "Frida" might be the embodiment of a whole new mourning and nostalgia for earlier times and more recognizable lives.

The recycling of the image of Frida across real and digital highways carries a legacy she could not have dreamed of, since technology was not part of culture then. Yet her interest in reproducing her face to be looked at by herself and others seems fulfilled by the newest modes of reproducing images for easier access, greater numbers of buyers, and private use in the home. The recent move toward privatizing companies and institutions may find an unexpected symbol of private life behind closed doors in Frida: both her diary and her art reveal what happened when the light of public life extinguished and personal living took over. Diego's wild nights on the town and very visible liaisons with women, and Frida's affairs in New York and Mexico City, had a flipside to them. After they reconciled on his birthday in 1940, whatever they agreed to or whatever qualms they put aside could still play out in the space of their homes. The very fact that they lived separately most of the time, and that Frida told Diego to stay at the studio when he claimed he was in the middle of a project and could not be disturbed, may be more visible on her face as a mask with tears (1945) than in any news report or public announcement. The diary proved another place where she could keep things secret and private, at least until her death.

The private face of Frida is available to the public around the world in many shapes and forms. One of the first recyclings of her image appears to share the political arena with other icons of revolution, such as Ché

Guevara. In posters, her face peers out from under a beret—except for Subcomandante Marcos, the symbol of the neo-Zapatistas since 1994 who wears a ski mask, the beret is a standard marker for revolutionaries—with a star centered on the front. This recalls Chinese youth under Mao up through the 1960s and almost any photo of Ché Guevara in Bolivia or in Cuba in the 1950s. A young Frida appears determined, staring straight ahead, hair cropped short and ornamental beads around her neck. She means business, and has little to do with her softer image in self-portraits. Perhaps, however, it is a question of the shared values of all revolutionaries, such as the musical competitors in Cuba in 2007, that allows her face to join the ranks of other inspirational leaders. In a vision of eternal youth, or perhaps of an enduring hope for change, Frida joins Ché and Eva Perón as icons of cultural loss—at the hands of the military, at the hands of cancer, at the hands of disease. A political agenda is only implicit; the real message is the medium that carries it.

Another legacy as recycled image is the face of Frida as an icon for books of Mexican recipes. Although a number of collections use her face to promote the genuine aspect of their contents, it may be more of a figurative symbol than a literal one. Like recipes for survival, food and Frida go hand-in-hand through the ages and promote a unique access to the "real" Mexico for those outside the culture. Both live on. In one case, a collection compiled by Marie Pierre Colle and Guadalupe Rivera, one of Diego Rivera's daughters, presents Frida's favorites in *Frida's Fiestas* (1994). A photograph of Frida's middle-aged face appears in one corner of the cover, with all kinds of vegetables and spices spread across the rest. These fiestas suggest a community brought together through food and, as the subtitle states, these are also "recipes and reminiscences of life with Frida Kahlo." There are two hot topics here: Mexican food as part of the fastest-growing immigrant community in the United States in the 1990s, and Frida as the face of authentic Mexico.

Not too far afield from other exported icons of so-called Mexicanness in the 1990s such as the film and novel *Like Water for Chocolate*, this cookbook places Frida among ears of corn, chiles, and other spices as another ingredient from nature to be mixed into a shared experience of cooking. Mexican women and women in global societies still share the kitchen as their space, it seems. The seventeenth-century Mexican nun Sor Juana Inés de la Cruz (1648–1695) became empowered in the kitchen as she turned it into a scientific lab of sorts for the production of philosophical knowledge more than food. The focus of a 1990 María Luisa Bemberg film on iconic women—*Yo la peor de todas* (I the Worst of All)—Sor Juana attempted to turn the tables on the church hierarchy even if she ultimately became its victim. She does not appear on t-shirts and altars, even though in the late 1990s her face began to grace the 1,000-peso banknote. With Frida back amid the pots and pans, the sauces such as *mole* and *pipián*, maybe Frida represents a nostalgic look back at a traditional space for women even as more and more Mexican women (and other women) go into the workforce. Cooking for Diego gave Frida a feeling of power and a way to communicate with him after he spent long days on the scaffold painting. Cooking today with recipes of many ingredients is more of a bridge to the past—as in Tita's case in *Like Water for Chocolate*—or a luxury.

Much has been written about Frida and frustrated maternity, about the so-called natural and inseparable link between women and biology which, when broken, yields an image such as the unmarried scholar nun Sor Juana Inés de la Cruz, or women militants handing out political flyers. Yet Eli Bartra suggests another way to look at this duality personified in the multiple clocks and timepieces available for sale with Frida's face on them. Bartra writes that, for the mythmaking muralists, "una mujer es madre o es puta, o es virgen o es adorno, punto" (a woman is a mother or a whore, she is a virgin or a decoration, end of story) (1994, 91). Kahlo as clock, then, shows a peculiar return to the old dichotomy of woman as biology or as adornment. This time around, the decoration is for all consumers, not just men. Frida goes from Diego's painting of the Alameda Park to today's modern *alacena* (kitchen cabinet) with ease. Clocks tell time on the face of a timeless woman.

All of the commercial products with Frida's face on them are part of a storytelling fantasy, really, since they allow the observer to state and restate what goes along with her image as part of the new object. A matchbook with a young Frida may open the door to speak of her optimism or her accident; an apron with a portrait at age 30 might resurrect tales of Diego's infidelity and her pain; a calendar with 12 Fridas marks the entire transition from beginning to end, with anecdotes about each stage in between; a tattoo could be with the wearer through the stages of life as a faithful companion. But there is another aspect of fantasy where she is even more appealing to the eye. As part of the front cover of a paperback collection of "the best stories of the fantastic" from the now-global publisher *Alfaguara*, a painting of a Frida look-alike stands among catfish with arms, winged dolphins, the remnants of a huge tree, and little devils to entice the reader into the world of the fantastic. Touted as a return to such magical literary treasures from a variety of countries, this anthology brings to the reader a sampling of what the prologue calls the equally fantastic realities of Spain, Colombia, Argentina, and the rest of the nations of the Spanish-speaking world. The prologue ends with a remark that these readings will offer a perverse pleasure, that of ripping apart bit by bit the reality that surrounds us (Benet and Estruch Tobella 2001, 9). As the Frida-like woman on the cover lifts her skirts to the knee to reveal stories by Gabriel García Márquez, Carlos Fuentes, Juan Rulfo, Juan José Millás, and of course Jorge Luis Borges, she also sets up the seduction of this ornament. On her legs are decorations and tattoos, treasures hidden by the traditional garb of her hair, dress, and jewelry. No real native, but a disguise with other secrets inside, the image works as a perfect symbol for Frida. Like her *Two Fridas* or her divided self-portrait on the border, the multiplicity of realities within one identity turn things into complicated, paradoxical stories ripe for fantasizing about. Perhaps the suggestion of Frida—that enigma personified—will help sell this book as much as the names of the writers contained inside.

One of the official policies of the United States government in the past couple of decades has been the championing of multiculturalism. Volumes have been written by academics and others about the dangers of homogenizing cultures into a blender of apolitical sameness, espousing the virtues of difference while not supporting the rights of the actual people who belong to the vast and varied societies and cultures making up today's national panoramas. Like the collective terms Hispanic or Latino, used to designate the somehow unified and universal heritage of Spanish-speaking cultures, multiculturalism appeared on the horizon more than a decade ago to spur exhibitions and clothing lines, foods and writers, academic panel discussions and college dormitory round tables.

So, when on May 21, 2001, the U.S. Postal Service announced its continued "Celebration of Fine Arts" with the release a month later of a commemorative stamp in honor of Frida Kahlo, some found it a moment of pride, for Frida would thus join the illustrious pantheon of stamp images alongside Elvis, B.B. King, Malcolm X., Mickey Mouse, Martin Luther King, Jr. and other notables. The first Hispanic woman to be honored with a U.S. postage stamp, and released to the eager public at the doors of the Phoenix Art Museum, she is an example of "those special people who have had a significant influence on American history, art, and culture." These words were uttered by Benjamin P. Ocasio, then Vice President of Diversity Development for the U.S. Postal Service, in honor of Frida Kahlo. Not quite 10 years following the implementation of the Free Trade Act, a folkloric Frida appears in a self-portrait on a U.S. stamp, ready to circulate freely across the borders others wait avidly to cross. That Frida Kahlo, a Mexican-Hungarian artist, would be celebrated in an official U.S. government program for her contributions across borders is a visionary act. Now this young, exotic-looking, short-haired, calm young woman with a long neck encircled with dark blue stone beads would take her place alongside Freddy Prince, Jr., Andy García, Jennifer López, Edward James Olmos, Raquel Welch, and other stars who have left their stamp on culture, as special people and Hispanics, whether from Puerto Rico or Cuba or Mexico. More intriguing, however, is that an announcement that Mexico would simultaneously release a stamp dedicated to Frida was retracted a few days later. A Mexican Frida stamp was never issued.

There was a round of controversy regarding the issuance of the U.S. Kahlo stamp based on the fact that Frida was not an American and reportedly had been a Communist. From what is known of her feelings toward the Party, this might have stirred Frida herself to respond as she did when relegated to typing speeches. A suggestion that Norman Rockwell, already celebrated in postage form, would be an infinitely better choice, was proposed but unheeded. After all of the films, books, exhibitions, and international attention she had received, Kahlo was still a mystery to many, an obscure riddle that each was invited to fill in as they wished. The stamp of Frida sold out quickly. She became a philatelic superstar.

Performance artists and craftspeople, some inspired by Frida's words and others by her art, continue to bring Frida back to life on stage and in museums and galleries. As another act in the drama of her life and legacy, some of the most recent news related to Frida Kahlo has to do with her being canonized as a saint. In the middle of the Mexico City Centennial exhibition, and one day before the commemoration of her death on July 13, 2007, it was reported that Frida was one step closer to sainthood. One hundred years after her birth, some were pushing for this to occur before more time went by, as she might be lost in the mists of history. In her support, several miracles have been attested to: one related to the birth of fame and talent in an actress who had previously lacked both but called upon Frida for help; another in the realm of the flexibility of political affiliations and the switching of parties à la Frida; a third called Frida a miraculous muse for a blocked writer who sat down and poured out hundreds of pages when she had been incapable of composing one. Whatever the outcome of this process, and without further comment on it, there is one foregone conclusion to all of the items and homages studied here: the afterlife of Frida has been remarkably profitable on the one hand, and extraordinarily enduring on the other.

SELECTED BIBLIOGRAPHY

Ades, Dawn. *Art in Latin America: The Modern Era, 1920–1980*. New Haven: Yale University Press, 1989.

Alcántara, Isabel, and Sandra Egnolff. *Frida Kahlo and Diego Rivera*. Munich: Prestel, 2005.

Ankori, Gannit. *Imaging Her Selves: Frida Kahlo's Poetics of Identity and Fragmentation*. Westport: Greenwood, 2002.

Baddeley, Oriana. "Her Dress Hangs Here: De-frocking the Kahlo Cult." *Oxford Art Journal* 14, no. 1 (1991): 10–17.

———, and Valerie Fraser. *Drawing the Line: Art and Cultural Identity in Contemporary Latin America*. London: Verso, New Left Books, the Latin American Bureau, 1989.

Baker, Kenneth. "Frida Kahlo: Tate Modern." *ARTnews* 104, no. 10 (Nov 2005): 193.

Barnet-Sánchez, Holly. "Frida Kahlo: Her Life and Art Revisited." *Latin American Research Review* 32, no. 3 (1997): 243–57.

Barrera, Norma Anabel. *Frida Kahlo y Diego Rivera*. Mexico City: Planeta, 2002.

Bartra, Eli. *Frida Kahlo: Mujer, Ideología y Arte*. Barcelona: Icaria, 1994.

Bauer, Claudia. *Frida Kahlo*. Translated by Stephen Telfer. Munich: Prestel, 2007.

Benet, Juan and Joan Estruch Tobella (eds.). *Los Mejores relatos fantásticos de habla hispanica*. Mexico City: Alfaguara, 2001.

Billeter, Erika, ed. *The World of Frida Kahlo: The Blue House*. Houston: Museum of Fine Arts, 1994.

Braverman, Kate. *The Incantation of Frida K.* New York: Seven Stories Press, 2002.

Breton, André. *Surrealism and Painting*. Translated by Michel Parmentier and Jacqueline d'Amboise. New York: Harper and Row, 1967.

Burrus, Christina. *Frida Kahlo: Painting Her Own Reality*. New York: Abrams, 2008.

Carnero, Guillermo. "Frida Kahlo: Folclore, Tradición y Vanguardia." *Cuadernos Hispanoamericanos* 688 (2007): 97.

Chadwick, Whitney. *Women Artists and the Surrealist Movement*. New York: Thames and Hudson and Little Brown, 1985.

Colle, Marie Pierre, Guadalupe Rivera, and Guadalupe Rivera Marín. *Frida's Fiestas: Recipes and Reminiscences of Life with Frida Kahlo*. Translated by Kenneth Krabbenhoft. New York: Clarkson Potter (Random House), 1994.

Conde, Teresa del. *Frida Kahlo: La Pintora y el Mito*. Mexico City: Plaza y Janés, 2001.

Dexter, Emma and Tanya Barson, eds. *Frida Kahlo*. London: Tate Publishing, 2005. Curators' catalogue to accompany the exhibition "Frida Kahlo" shown at the Tate Modern.

Drucker, Malka. *Frida Kahlo*. Albuquerque: University of New Mexico Press, 1995.

Franco, Jean. *Plotting Women: Gender and Representation in Mexico*. New York: Columbia University Press, 1991.

Frida Kahlo: The Camera Seduced. Memoir by Elena Poniatowska. Essay by Carla Stellweg. San Francisco: Chronicle Books, 1992.

Fuentes, Carlos. "Introduction." *The Diary of Frida Kahlo: An Intimate Self-Portrait*. New York: Harry Abrams, 2005.

Goldman, Shifra M. *Dimensions of the Americas: Art and Social Change in Latin America and the United States*. Chicago: University of Chicago Press, 1995.

———. "Six Women Artists of Mexico." *Women's Art Journal*. 3 (Fall 1982/Winter 1983): 1–9.

Grimberg, Salomon. *Frida Kahlo: Song of Herself*. London, New York: Merrell, 2008.

———. *I Will Never Forget You: Frida Kahlo & Nickolas Muray: Unpublished Photographs and Letters*. San Francisco: Chronicle, 2006.

———. *Lola Alvarez Bravo: The Frida Kahlo Photographs*. Dallas: The Texas Society of the Friends of Mexican Culture, 1991.

———, James Oles, Carlos Fuentes, and Raquel Tibol. *Frida Kahlo: National Homage 1907–2007*. Mexico City: Instituto Nacional de Bellas Artes, 2007. An exhibition catalogue.

Havard, Lucy Ann. "Frida Kahlo, Mexicanidad and Máscaras: The Search for Identity in Postcolonial Mexico." *Romance Studies* 24, no. 3 (2006): 241–51.

Herrera, Hayden. *Frida*. New York: Newmarket Press, 2002.

———. *Frida: A Biography of Frida Kahlo*. New York: Harper and Row, 1983.

———. *Frida Kahlo*. New York: Rizzoli, 1992.

———. *Frida Kahlo: A Life of Passion*. New York: Harper and Row, 1997.

———. *Frida Kahlo: The Paintings*. New York: Harper Perennial, 1993.

———, and Salomon Grimberg. *Frida Kahlo. The Still Lifes*. New York: Merrell, 2008.

———, Víctor Zamudio Taylor, Elizabeth Carpenter, and Kathy Halbreich. *Frida Kahlo*. Minneapolis: Walker Art Center, 2007.

Kahlo, Frida, Carlos Fuentes, and Sarah M. Lowe. *The Diary of Frida Kahlo: An Intimate Self-Portrait*. New York: Harry Abrams, 2005.

———, and Raquel Tibol. *Frida by Frida*. Mexico RM Publishers, 2003.

Kahlo, Guillermo. *Mexiko 1904*. Mexico City: Universidad Iberoamericana, 2006.

Kahlo, Isolda P. *Frida Íntima (1907–1954)*. Mexico City: Ediciones Dipon and Ediciones Gato Azul, 2004.

Kulish, Nancy. "Frida Kahlo and Object Choice: A Daughter the Rest of Her Life." *Psychoanalytic Inquiry* 1 (Jan–March 2006): 7.

Lindauer, Margaret. *Devouring Frida: The Art History and Popular Celebrity of Frida Kahlo*. Middletown: Wesleyan University Press, 1999.

Maiz-Peña, Magdalena. "Cuerpo Fotográfico, Subjetividad(es) y Representación Visual: Lola Alvarez Bravo y Frida Kahlo." *Studies in Latin American Popular Culture* 22 (2003): 193–206.

Mujica, Barbara. *Frida*. Woodstock, New York: Overlook Press, 2001.

Mulvey, Laura, and Peter Wollen. *Frida Kahlo and Tina Modotti*. London: Whitechapel Art Gallery, 1982.

Newhall, E. "Frida Kahlo." *ARTnews* 107, no. 5 (2008): 154.

Prignitz-Poda, Helga. *Frida Kahlo: Life and Work*. New York: Schirmer, 2007.

Rico, Araceli. *Frida Kahlo: Fantasía de un Cuerpo Herido*. Mexico City: Plaza y Janés, 1987.

Rummel, Jack. *Frida Kahlo: A Spiritual Biography*. New York: Crossroad Publishing, 2000.

Schaefer, Claudia. *Textured Lives: Women, Art, and Representation in Modern Mexico*. Tucson: University of Arizona Press, 1991.

Schwartz, S. "The Nerve of Frida Kahlo." *New York Review of Books* 55, no.8 (2008): 4.

Sheridan, Guillermo. "Frida Kahlo Más Cerca de los Altares." *Letras Libres* (August 2007), http://www.letraslibres.com/.

Sussman, Erika, and Loha Marconi. "Channeling Frida." *Florida International Magazine* 8, no. 9 (October 2005): 104–113.

Tibol, Raquel. *Escrituras de Frida Kahlo*. Selection and notes by Raquel Tibol. Prologue by Antonio Alatorre. Mexico City: Plaza y Janés and CONACULTA, 1999.

———. *Frida Kahlo: An Open Life*. Translated by Elinor Randall. Albuquerque: University of New Mexico Press, 1993.

Zamora, Martha. *Frida: El Pincel de la Angustia*. Mexico City: Martha Zamora and Laboratorio Lito Color, S.A., 1987.

INDEX

About the Author

CLAUDIA SCHAEFER is a Professor of Spanish and Chair of the Department of Modern Languages and Cultures at the University of Rochester, New York.

Recent Titles in Greenwood Biographies

Eleanor Roosevelt: A Biography
Cynthia M. Harris

Jesse Owens: A Biography
Jacqueline Edmondson

The Notorious B.I.G.: A Biography
Holly Lang

Hillary Clinton: A Biography
Dena B. Levy and Nicole R. Krassas

Johnny Depp: A Biography
Michael Blitz

Judy Blume: A Biography
Kathleen Tracy

Nelson Mandela: A Biography
Peter Limb

LeBron James: A Biography
Lew Freedman

Tecumseh: A Biography
Amy H. Sturgis

Diana, Princess of Wales: A Biography
Martin Gitlin

Nancy Pelosi: A Biography
Elaine S. Povich

Barack Obama: A Biography
JoAnn F. Price

Sacagawea: A Biography
April R. Summitt